CW00418818

A REVOLUTIONARY ARMY

I n 1914 the multinational Russian Empire, with a population of about 167 million spread over a land area of 8.45 million square miles, encompassed the present-day Russian Federation, most of Poland, Finland, the Baltic states (Estonia, Latvia, Lithuania), Byelorussia, Ukraine, Moldova, Transcaucasia (Armenia, Georgia and Azerbaijan) and Central Asia (Kazakhstan, Turkmenistan, Uzbekistan, Tajikistan and Kyrgystan). Its political system was unstable, as Tsar Nicholas II resisted demands for increased democracy.

In the Great War, the 5 million-strong Russian Imperial Army proved unable to stem the German and Austrian advances. Riots in the capital St Petersburg (later, Leningrad) led to the 'February Revolution' of 7 March 1917 (23 February OS)[1], the Tsar's abdication, and the establishment of a Provisional Government. This was followed on 7 November 1917 (25 October OS) by the 'October Revolution', when Vladimir Ilich Lenin's Bolshevik Party proclaimed a Russian Republic.

The state was renamed on 28 January 1918 as the Russian Soviet Federative Socialist Republic (RSFSR). On 30 December 1922 it was joined by the Byelorussian, Ukrainian and Transcaucasian (later Armenian, Azerbaijan and Georgian) Soviet Socialist Republics (SSRs), to form the Union of Soviet Socialist Republics (USSR – 'Soviet Union'). Additional SSRs were steadily incorporated: Turkmen and Uzbek, 13 May 1925; Tadjik, 5 December 1929; Kazakh and Kirgiz, 5 December 1936; Moldavian, 2 August 1940; and Lithuanian, Latvian and Estonian, 3–6 August 1940, making a total of 15 Soviet Republics.[2]

To consolidate Bolshevik power, in March 1917 Lenin formed the Red Guard (*Krasnaya Gvardiya*) as a 200,000-strong workers' militia. On 28 January 1918 the Workers' and Peasants' Red Army (*Raboche-Krest'yanskaya Krasnaya Armiya* – RKKA), comprising Land Forces and Air Force, and on 11 February the Red Fleet (RKKF), were established as the armed forces of the Bolshevik Revolution, supported by the *Cheka* internal

A confident officer cadet at a Tank School, 1939. He wears the light 'steel-grey' Armoured Troops officer's service cap and field shirt, with an M32 field belt and crossbrace. His collar patches are those of a private, and have the brass tank branch badges applied at a non-regulation angle. (Tshakov Collection)

1 Until 1918 Russia used the 'Old Style' Julian Calendar, 13 days behind the Gregorian Calendar.
2 For the complex partition of Ukraine, see MAA 412: *Ukrainian Armies 1914–55*.

security organization, formed 20 December 1917. Red forces were victorious against the ex-Imperial/Provisional government White Russian armies, Allied interventionist troops and nationalist forces in the Russian Civil War, 7 November 1917–25 October 1922. After this, Finland and the Baltic States won independence, Bessarabia joined Rumania, and Poland occupied western Belarus and western Ukraine (18 March 1921) after the Polish-Soviet War. The Bolshevik state had survived, but was surrounded by potential enemies and felt vulnerable to attack.

From 1922, Soviet forces fought internal threats, particularly the Central Asian *Basmachi* rebellion of October 1922–June 1931. Later the Soviet government sent equipment and a 3,000-strong military mission to support the Republicans in the Spanish Civil War, July 1936–April 1939. The greatest external threat was in the Far Eastern Region, with armed incursions by Chinese and White Russian forces from Manchuria in October–December 1929. Japan, with an army established in Manchuria, coveted the Far Eastern Region and Eastern Siberia, and the Soviet Union sent equipment and a 3,600-man military mission (replacing a German mission) to support Chinese Nationalists fighting the Japanese in October 1937–September 1939. In a major escalation of Soviet-Japanese hostilities, the 22,950-strong 39th Rifle Corps and 2nd Mechanized Brigade blocked Japanese incursions on the Manchukuo-Russian border near Lake Khasan in the 'Changkufeng Incident' of July–August 1938. This was followed by the battle of Khalkha River (Khalkin-Gol) in May–August 1939, when the Soviet-Mongolian 1st Army Group under *Komkor* G.K. Zhukov defeated Japanese Kwantung Army units claiming a Soviet border zone.

THE SOVIET HIGH COMMAND

The Soviet Union was a totalitarian state, with the Marxist-Leninist Communist Party as the only legal political party. The chief executive was the Chairman of the Communist Party, a post held 3 April 1922–5 March 1953 by Iosif Vissarionovich Dzhugashvili, alias Stalin, 'Man of Steel'. The most gifted Red Army officer of the pre-war period was undoubtedly Mikhail Nikolayevich Tukhachevsky, who as Deputy People's Commissar for Defence and Head of the Red Army's Technology and Armament Department (July 1931–April 1936) transformed a mass infantry and cavalry militia into the most modern mechanized army in the world.

Stalin, however, being determined to monopolize all state power, imprisoned and executed actual or suspected political opponents from September 1932 in the 'Purges', culminating in the 'Great Purge' (October 1936–October 1938). More than 6.5 million people were 'eliminated', including 434 (64 per cent) of the Red Army's 684 general officers; *Marshal Sovetskogo Soyuza* Tukhachevsky was executed as a suspected German spy on 11 June 1937. The Red Army had been decapitated, leaving large formations commanded by generals who were

Stalin (left) with Kliment Voroshilov, People's Commissar for Defence – i.e. defence minister – in 1938. Until March 1943, Stalin wore a grey service cap, closed-collar tunic and trousers, without military insignia. Voroshilov wears the grey M35 service uniform of a *marshal Sovetskogo Soyuza*. (Tshakov Collection)

World War II Soviet Armed Forces (1)

1939–41

Dr Nigel Thomas • Illustrated by Darko Pavlovic

Series editor Martin Windrow

First published in Great Britain in 2010 by Osprey Publishing,
PO Box 883, Oxford, OX1 9PL, UK
PO Box 3985, New York, NY 10185-3985, USA
Email: info@ospreypublishing.com

Osprey Publishing is part of the Osprey Group.

Transferred to digital print on demand 2014.

First published 2010
2nd impression 2013

Printed and bound in Great Britain

A CIP catalogue record for this book is available from the British Library.

ISBN: 978 184908 400 0
ebook ISBN: 978 1 84908 401 7

Editorial by Martin Windrow
Page layouts by Myriam Bell Design, France
Typeset in Helvetica Neue and ITC New Baskerville
Index by Michael Forder
Originated by PPS Grasmere Ltd, Leeds, UK

Acknowledgements
Nigel Thomas would like to thank Ventsislav Chakov, Nik Cornish, László Pál Szabó and
Pierre C.T. Verheye for their assistance and inspiration, and also his wife Heather for her
tireless encouragement and support. He would also like to acknowledge his debt to the
writings of László Békési, Aleksandr Kibovskiy, Chris Nelson, Jan Rutkiewicz, Aleksey
Stepanov, Kirill Tsiplenkov, David Webster and Steven Zaloga.

Artist's note
Readers may care to note that the original paintings from which the colour plates in this
book were prepared are available for private sale. All reproduction copyright whatsoever
is retained by the Publishers. All enquiries should be addressed to:

Darko Pavlovíc, Modecova 3, Zagreb 10090, Croatia

The Publishers regret that they can enter into no correspondence upon this matter.

The Woodland Trust
Osprey Publishing is supporting the Woodland Trust, the UK's leading woodland
conservation charity, by funding the dedication of trees.

www.ospreypublishing.com

The victors over the Japanese at Khalkin-Gol, 1939. (Left to right) *Komandarm 1-go ranga* Grigoriy Shtern, commanding 1st Independent Red Banner Army; the Mongolian prime minister, Marshal of the Mongolian People's Republic Khorloogiyn Choybalsan; and *Komkor* Georgiy Zhukov, 1st Army Group. The Mongolian Army wore Red Army M35 uniforms with Mongolian M36 rank insignia on collar patches, and Soviet-style M22 cuff patches. (Tshakov Collection)

mostly bureaucratic yes-men, intimidated by political commissars, and lacking initiative and battle experience. Tukhachevsky's vision was fatally compromised, and the Red Army paid dearly in lives and territory for its inadequate performance against Finland in November 1939 and the Axis in June 1941 – events that triggered a second series of purges of senior officers between October 1940 and February 1942.

Control of the Armed Forces was exercised by the cabinet or Council of People's Commissars (*Sovet Narodnnykh Komissarov* – Sovnarkom), chaired by Stalin; a 'People's Commissar' was a minister. Sovnarkom included the People's Commissariat for Defence, under a general officer: from 20 June 1934, *Komandarm* Kliment Yefremovich Voroshilov; from 7 May 1940, *Marshal Sovetskogo Soyuza* Semyon Konstantinovich Timoshenko, and from 19 July 1941 Stalin himself. In peacetime this office controlled the Chief of General Staff: from May 1937, *Komandarm 1-go ranga* Boris Mikhailovitch Shaposhnikov; from August 1940, *Komandarm 1-go ranga* Kirill Afanasievich Meretskov; from 1 February 1941, *General Armii* Georgiy Konstantinovich Zhukov, and from July 1941 *Marshal Sovetskogo Soyuza* Shaposhnikov.

Stavka

On 23 June 1941, the day after the German attack on the Soviet Union, Stalin revived the general headquarters that had been discontinued since Tsarist days. The GHQ of the High Command of the Armed Forces of the USSR (*Stavka Glavnogo Komandovaniya Vooruzhennykh Sil SSSR*) was chaired by the People's Commissar for Defence (Timoshenko, then Stalin), and comprised the most senior military, internal security and political leaders. The Stavka effectively supplanted the People's Commissariat for Defence, co-ordinating the Soviet war effort through the General Staff. It was redesignated as GHQ of the Supreme Command (*Stavka Verkhovnogo Komandovaniya*) on 10 July 1941, and as GHQ of the Supreme High Command (*Stavka Verkhovnogo Glavnokomandovaniya*) on

20 November 1935: the five general officers created Marshals of the Soviet Union on that date. Their careers, and indeed their lives, were entirely dependent upon Stalin's favour. (Standing:) Budyonny – a brave but unimaginative cavalryman promoted far beyond his competence, who survived to die in retirement in 1973; Blyukher – shot in 1938. (Seated:) Tukachevsky – architect of the modernized Red Army, shot in 1937; Voroshilov – died in retirement in 1969; and Yegorov – died in prison in 1939. (Tshakov Collection)

8 August 1941. Military-civilian liaison was achieved by the establishment from 30 June 1941 of the State Committee for Defence (*Gosudarstvenniy Komitet Oborony* – GKO), chaired by Stalin.

RED ARMY LAND FORCES

Lenin had envisaged the RKKA as a mass levy reflecting Marxist-Leninist principles, favouring the urban and rural working class against the aristocracy and middle classes, and representing a complete break with Russian military and nationalist traditions. Tukhachevsky had turned it into a formidable mechanized fighting force, but this was fatally weakened by the Great Purge. In September 1939 the official title was abbreviated to Red Army (*Krasnaya Armiya* – KA), divided into the Land Forces (*Sukhoputnye Voyska*), and the Red Army Military Air Force (*Voenno-Vozdushnye Sily Krasnoy Armii* – VVS-KA). For simplicity, in this text the term 'Red Army' refers to the Land Forces unless otherwise stated.

Personnel

Boys received elementary pre-military training at schools from 12 to 18 years. Under the 'Stalin Constitution' of 5 December 1936, men aged 21 (reduced in 1939 to 19, and from June 1941 to 18) either served for two years in the Land Forces and then transferred to the Territorial Army under Army Reserve officers, or served in the Territorial Army for 8–11 months spread over five years. All soldiers were liable for call-up until age 50, but in wartime they served until the end of hostilities. Non-commissioned officers were mainly conscripts trained at the unit Regimental School (*Polkovaya Shkola*), with re-enlisted NCOs filling the higher ranks. This was essentially a Tsarist system, which prevented the emergence of an effective NCO corps.

An 18-year old civilian or promising NCO could be appointed officer cadet (*kursant*) and sent to a branch-specific Military School (*Voennaya Shkola*) – renamed 1939 Military College (*Voennoe Uchilishche*) – for three years' training (four years for other services), reduced in the wartime panic from 25 June 1941 to just 4–10 months. He was commissioned *leytenant*, from 5 August 1937 *mladshiy leytenant*, continuing as a regular officer or transferring to the Army Reserve. Regular captains and majors could be selected for three years' study at a branch-specific Military Academy (*Voennaya Akademiya*) before further promotion, and later for two years at the General Staff Academy (*Voennaya Akademiya General'nogo Shtaba*) – in operation from April 1936 to May 1940 – to fit them for promotion to field and general officer ranks respectively.

Marshal Timoshenko (right), commanding Western Strategic Direction, briefs his Front commanders, with a staff *mayor* (second left) in attendance. (Left) *General Polkovnik* Fedor Isidorovich Kuznetzov, Central Front; (second right) *General Armii* Dmitriy Nikolaevich Pavlov, Western Front. (Tshakov Collection)

Land Forces branches, 10 March 1936–31 December 1941

The Red Army (excluding the Air Force) comprised 19 branches from March 1936, growing to 21 branches by December 1941. These were divided into eight groups – six combat arms, services, and specialist officers – as follows:

(1) Infantry. The largest arm, it comprised Rifle Regiments ('Rifles' had formerly designated élite Tsarist infantry); Mechanized Battalions; Motorized Rifle ('Motor Rifle') Regts/Bns (1939); Mountain Rifle Regts; and Machine-Gun Battalions.

(2) Cavalry. An obsolescent branch since 1914, mounted troops were nevertheless still effective in open steppe country against infantry. It comprised Cavalry Regts; Cossack Regts (from 23 April 1936); and Mountain Cavalry Regiments.

(3) Armoured Troops. These comprised Tank Regts/Bns/ Companies; Reconnaissance Bns/Coys; and (from 1940) Motorcycle Regiments.

(4) Artillery, providing infantry support with Super-Heavy Artillery Regts; Heavy Artillery Regts/Bns; Field Artillery Regts, Howitzer Regts, Rocket-Launcher Regts/Bns; Mortar Bns; Anti-Aircraft Bns; and Horse Artillery Battalions.

(5) Technical Troops included Engineer Bns/Coys; Electrical Engineer Maintenance Bns; Ordnance Bns; Pontoon Engineer Bns (for bridging); Construction Engineer and Road Maintenance Engineer ('Sapper') Bns/Coys; Railway Engineer Bns; Signal Bns/Coys; Motor Transport Bns/Coys; Military Transport and Railway Troops (31 August 1936).

(6) Chemical Troops, comprising Flamethrower Bns and anti-gas Chemical Companies.

(7) Services. These included the Supply and Administration Service; Medical Service, providing Medical Bns and Field Hospitals;

July 1941: a *starshiy leytenant* of engineers demonstrates the M1891/30 rifle to a platoon of the People's Militia (NO) in Moscow or Leningrad. The officer wears M35 khaki service uniform, with black collar patches piped gold and bearing the crossed-axes branch badge. By September 1941 these militiamen were in Red Army uniforms and deployed in rifle divisions. (Nik Cornish Collection)

and Veterinary Service, with Veterinary Hospitals.

(8) Specialist Officers. Those who could be attached to units of any arm were Technical Officers, Legal Officers and Bandmasters. Political Officers or Commissars ensured that unit commanders obeyed the Communist Party line. Downgraded from 1925 under Tukhachevsky, they were reinstated from 10 May 1937 during Stalin's purges; abolished in August 1940; and reinstated in July 1941, following Soviet defeats. Hitler's notorious 'Commissar Order' (*Kommissarbefehl*) of 6 June 1941 demanded immediate execution for political officers taken prisoner, thereby in fact stiffening Red Army resistance.

Winter War, February 1940: two infantrymen – probably snipers – wearing M31 'Finnish' fleece caps and white cotton snow-camouflage hooded coats, and carrying the new SVT-40 semi-automatic rifle. They are being briefed by a *kapitan* company commander, wearing an M27 *budyonovka* field cap and a khaki quilted *telogreika* overjacket, with M35 infantry collar patches. (Nik Cornish Collection)

ORGANIZATION OF LAND FORCES, JULY 1939–31 DECEMBER 1941

Military Districts

A Military District (*Voennyi Okrug*) comprised a number of field armies, corps, divisions and other units. It was usually commanded by a *komandarm*, from 13 July 1940 a *general armii – general mayor* (see Table 4 for rank sequence). The Soviet Union was divided into 18 Military Districts:

European RSFSR – Arkhangel'sk, formed 26 March 1940; Kalinin, 17 November 1940; Leningrad, Moscow, Orel, and North Caucasus; Baltic (Estonia, Latvia, Lithuania), 11 July 1940; Byelorussian; Ukraine – Kharkov, Kiev and Odessa; Transcaucasian (Armenia, Georgia, Azerbaijan); Central Asia.

Asiatic RSFSR – Far Eastern, Siberian, Transbaikal, Ural, Volga.

The three western border districts were redesignated Special Military Districts: Kiev (26 July 1938), Byelorussian (11 July 1940) and Baltic (17 August 1940).

Strategic Directions

Three Strategic Direction HQs were formed 10 July 1941, but were never accorded real authority and were soon abolished. Each Strategic Direction (*Strategicheskoe Napravleni*) controlled a number of Fronts under a *marshal Sovetskogo Soyuza* reporting directly to Stavka:

North-Western Direction (Northern and North-Western Fronts), under Voroshilov, facing German Army Group North; abolished August 1941.

Western Direction (Central, Reserve and Western Fronts), under Timoshenko, against Army Group Centre; abolished September 1941.

South-Western Direction (South-Western and Southern), under Budyonny, later Timoshenko, facing Army Group South; abolished September 1941.

Fronts

In wartime a Military District formed an army group called a *Front*, typically with two to five armies plus corps and smaller units, including a strong Air Force contingent, under a *komandarm* or *komdiv*, *general armii* or *general mayor*. The Byelorussian and Ukrainian fronts were raised for the occupation of Eastern Poland (September–October 1939); thereafter fronts – such as North-Western Front, formed for the Winter War with Finland (November 1939–March 1940) – were permanent wartime formations, remaining in being until 2 September 1945.

To confront the Axis invasion of June 1941, eight military districts in Byelorussia, Ukraine, the Baltic, Transcaucasia and European Russia had formed 13 fronts by December 1941: Bryansk (re-formed December 1941), Central, Kalinin, Northern (split August 1941 into Karelian and Leningrad), North-Western, Reserve, Southern, South-Western, Transcaucasian (redesignated December 1941 as Caucasus), Volkhov, and Western (see Table 1). Far Eastern Front (formed 14 January 1941 from 1st and 2nd Independent Red Banner Armies) guarded the Soviet-Chinese border against Japanese incursions. Stavka also kept some armies as GHQ Reserve (RVGK) forces, to reinforce embattled fronts.

Armies

A field army (*armiya*), commanded by a *komandarm* or *komdiv*, later *general leytenant* or *general mayor*, was the basic strategic formation. Each military district raised up to five armies, to defend the home district or transfer to other districts under threat. Sixty armies (designated by numbers 3rd–61st, and Coastal) were in existence in September 1939–December 1941. Of these, 13 (3–15) were formed in 1939 for the Polish, Finnish and Bessarabian campaigns; two (25, 35) garrisoned the Far Eastern Military District against Japanese attack, with two (17, 36) in reserve in

Table 1: Red Army Fronts and Armies, 17 September 1939–31 December 1941

Front	Military District	Front Formation to 31.12.1941	Front Strategic Operations to 31.12.1941	Armies constituting the Front to 31.12.1941
Byelorussian	Byelorussian	17.9.39 – 25.9.39	Poland	3, 4, 10, 11
Ukrainian	Kiev Special	17.9.39 – 2.10.39	Poland	5, 6, 12
North-Western	Leningrad	12.1939 – 13.3.40.	Finland, Karelia	7–9, 13–15, 57, 59
– North-Western reformed	Baltic Special	22.6.41 – 31.12.41	Baltic States, Leningrad, Tikhvin	8, 11, 27/4S, 34, 60/3S
Northern	Leningrad	24.6.41 – 23.8.41	Karelia, Leningrad	7, 8, 14, 23, 48, ALNO
Karelian	Leningrad	23.8.41 – 31.12.41	Karelia	7, 14, 58, 59
Leningrad	Leningrad	23.8.41 – 31.12.41	Leningrad, Tikhvin	8, 23, 42, 54, 55
Volkhov	Western Special	17.12.41 – 31.12.41	Tikhvin	4, 52
Western	Byelorussian	22.6.41 – 31.12.41	W.Byelorussia, Moscow	3-5, 10, 13, 16, 19/1S, 20, 24, 28–33, 43, 49, 50
Kalinin	Kalinin	17.10.41 – 31.12.41	Moscow	22, 29, 30, 31, 39, 41
Central	Western	24.7.41 – 25. 8.41	Smolensk, Kiev	3, 13, 21
Reserve	various	30.7.41 – 10.10.41	Smolensk, Moscow	24, 28–32, 34
Bryansk	Western Special	16.8.41 – 10. 11.41	Smolensk	3, 13, 21, 50
– Bryansk reformed	Western Special	18.12.41 – 31.12.41	Moscow	3, 13, 61
Southern	Moscow, Odessa	6.40 – 31.12.41	Bessarabia, W.Ukraine, Kiev, Donbass	5, 6, 9, 12, 18, 56, 57, Coastal
South-Western	Kiev Special	22.6.41 – 31.12.41	W.Ukraine, Kiev, Donbass, Moscow	3, 5, 6, 12, 13, 16, 19/1S, 21, 26/2S, 30, 37, 38, 40, 52, 56
Transcaucasian	Transcaucasian	23.8.41 – 29.12.41	Iran, Kerch-Feodosiya	44–47, 51, 53
Caucasus	Transcaucasian	30.12.41 – 31.12.41	Kerch-Feodosiya	44, 47, 51
Far Eastern	Far Eastern	28.6.38 – 31.12.41	-	1, 2

Khalkin-Gol, July 1939: *Polkovnik I.I. Fedyuninskiy*, commander of 24th Motor Rifle Brigade, 36th Motor Rifle Division. He wears the officers' light khaki cotton M35 summer field uniform, with a piped *pilotka* sidecap and *gymnastiorka* field shirt, and infantry collar patches and cuff chevrons displaying his rank: three bars, and one medium-width red chevron edged gold. His awards include the 20 Years' Service Medal. (Tshakov Collection)

Transbaikal. Thus 43 armies (16, 18–24, 26–34, 37–61, Coastal) were allocated to fight the Axis.

An army's establishment in 1941 usually comprised an HQ; Army HQ Troops including three regiments (replacement, engineer and signals) and 12–14 battalions (two reconnaissance, security, two engineer construction, road maintenance engineer, ordnance, two-four motor transport, chemical, flamethrower and penal); plus one-three corps under command. Six originally 'independent' armies (7, 9, 51, 56, 57, Coastal) were later allocated to fronts.

There were also four types of specialist army. In November–December 1941 four (19, 26, 60, 27) were redesignated as élite 'Shock Armies' (renumbered respectively 1–4), in GHQ Reserve ready to spearhead assaults on enemy lines; a Shock Army (*Udarnaya Armiya*) was reinforced with extra tank units. 1st Cavalry Army (*1-ya Konnaya Armiya*), a distinguished Civil War survivor, retained mounted cavalry corps in the Far Eastern Front. Ten 'Construction Engineer' armies (1–10) were formed 13 October 1941 to build defensive works around Moscow, Leningrad and other endangered cities, but were broken up February–October 1942 into smaller elements. A Construction Engineer Army (*Sapernaya Armiya*), 40–50,000 strong, comprised two-four sapper brigades, each with 19x 497-man battalions. Finally, Tsarist-style 'People's Militia' (*Narodnoe Opolcheniye* – NO) divisions were re-formed to defend Moscow and Leningrad in July 1941; the 16 Moscow divisions formed three armies (32–34) in September 1941, while the 11 Leningrad People's Militia Army (ALNO) divisions were reallocated to local Red Army formations.

Corps

There were 109 corps: 62 Rifle, 3 Territorial Rifle, 7 Cavalry, 5 Tank, 1 Special and 31 Mechanized, each under a *komdiv* or *kombrig*, later a *general mayor*.

A field army required three rifle corps; but due to the massive mobilization in June 1941, the shortage of qualified generals after the Great Purge, and the speed of the Axis advance, in fact only about 62 (numbered 1–62) of the 180-odd corps HQs required were actually formed. Consequently, Stavka abolished corps HQs on 15 July 1941, leaving each hard-pressed army commander to control nine rifle and other divisions directly. (Six corps HQs in fact survived, mainly in the Far Eastern Front.)

A 26,500-strong Rifle Corps (*Strelkoviy Korpus*) typically comprised a Corps HQ; Corps HQ Troops including two field artillery regiments, a reconnaissance company, and four battalions (engineer, signals, medical, and machine-gun); plus two-three rifle or other type divisions. In June 1940 the three formerly independent Baltic armies and air forces were redesignated as second-line Territorial Rifle corps of the Red Army – 22nd Estonian, 24th Latvian and 29th Lithuanian. Following mass desertions in June 1941, these corps were disbanded in Asiatic RSFSR; the officers were sent to die in labour camps and the other ranks transferred to penal battalions.

There were seven Cavalry corps (numbered 1–7), with 19,000 personnel each (i.e. only slightly larger than a rifle division). A Cavalry Corps (*Kavaleriyskiy Korpus*) comprised a Corps HQ; Corps HQ Troops, including four-six regiments (two-four tank, artillery, motorized heavy mortar) and other units; plus two-three cavalry or mountain cavalry divisions.

Five Tank corps (numbered 5, 10, 15, 20, 25) were formed in 1938, and four saw action pre-war: 20th in Khalkin-Gol, 15th and 25th in Eastern Poland, and 10th in Finland. An M38 Tank Corps (*Tankoviy Korpus*) had 12,710 men in an HQ; three battalions of Corps HQ Troops (reconnaissance, motor rifle, signals); plus one motor-rifle machine-gun and two light tank brigades, totalling 278 BT fast and 267 T-26 light tanks. (Armoured performance in Poland was deemed unsatisfactory, and the tank corps HQs were deactivated in November 1939.)

1st Mechanized Corps, the first such formation in the world, had been formed in 1932, and at least three others followed. 57th Special Corps, a mechanized formation, fought at Khalkin-Gol, but in September 1939 all mechanized corps HQs were deactivated. Eight corps (1-8) were re-formed in June 1940, reaching 31 (numbered 1-30, 39) by June 1941. A 37,200-strong M40 Mechanized Corps (*Mechanizyrovanniy Korpus*) had a Corps HQ; Corps HQ Troops (motorcycle regiment, motorized engineer battalion, signals battalion, aircraft flight); plus one motorized and two tank divisions. These corps – equipped with 1,108 KV heavy, T-34 medium and T-36 and T-37 light tanks, but poorly led, and lacking sufficient radio communications – were no match for the German Panzer divisions, and the remaining corps HQs were deactivated from 15 July 1941.

Guards formations

On 18 September 1941, as Axis forces advanced steadily towards Moscow, Stavka reintroduced the Tsarist élite designation of 'Guards' (*Gvardiya*) as an honour-title for award to distinguished formations up to army level. Guards units received special flags, and from 21 May 1942 personnel wore a prestigious breast-badge and had their personal ranks prefixed 'Guards'. Six Guards corps (three rifle, three cavalry) and 16 Guards divisions (10 rifle, 2 motorized, 4 cavalry) had been created by 31 December 1941. Guards formations were renumbered, and are listed hereafter in this text with their pre-Guards number (if any) in brackets; e.g., the three new

Khalkin-Gol, July 1939: personnel of 9th Tank Brigade with their M32 BA-10 armoured car. They wear M38 *panama* field hats with the M22 cap badge on a branch-colour cloth backing star, and enlisted ranks' M35 khaki field shirts. Note that rank and branch insignia have been removed from their Armoured Troops collar patches. The soldier at the right carries both the SM-1 gasmask bag on a wide sling, and a mapcase. (Tshakov Collection)

Guards cavalry corps were designated 1st (formerly 2nd Cavalry Corps), 2nd (ex-3rd), and 3rd (ex-5th).

Divisions: Rifle

About 571 divisions existed July 1939–December 1941, each under a *kombrig* or *polkovnik*, later a *general mayor* or *polkovnik*. Most of the divisions committed to battle were destroyed and re-formed, sometimes several times.

The Rifle Division (*Strelkovaya Diviziya*) was the backbone of the Red Army, and 374 had been formed by 31 December 1941: these were numbered 1–8, 10–14, 16–19, 21–27, 29, 31–35, 37–43, 45, 46, 49–56, 59–62, 64–67, 70–75, 78, 80, 84–94, 97–100, 102, 104, 105, 107, 108, 110–137, 140–162, 164–172, 174–191, 193, 195–197, 199–201, 203, 206, 207, 211, 212, 214, 215, 217, 218, 221–235, 237–241, 243–265, 267–301, 303–317, 320–396, 398, 400–402, 404, 406, 407, 409, 411, 413, 415, 416, 421–428, 430, 431, 434–6, 443 and 473. Ten divisions were subsequently redesignated Guards Rifle Divisions: 1st (formerly 100th), 2nd (127th), 3rd (153rd), 4th (161st), 5th (107th), 6th (120th), 7th (64th), 8th (316th), 9th (78th), and 10th (52nd).

An M39 Rifle Division (introduced September 1939) had 18,841 personnel, in the HQ; six battalions of HQ Troops (reconnaissance – with a light tank company, cavalry squadron, and self-propelled artillery battery; anti-aircraft, anti-tank, engineers, signals, and medical) and four HQ Troops companies (supply, maintenance, field and veterinary hospitals); plus one light and one medium artillery regiment (three 3-battery battalions each), and three rifle regiments. A Rifle Regiment (numbered in the 1–1,375 series) had an HQ; AA, infantry gun, AT and mortar batteries; reconnaissance, engineer, and signal companies; and three rifle battalions. A Rifle Battalion had an AT platoon, machine-gun (12x Maxim M1910 heavy MGs) and mortar companies, and three rifle companies. Each rifle company had an MG platoon (2x heavy MGs), and three rifle platoons each with four sections of 12 men. The M40 Rifle Division (13 June 1940) had slightly changed allocations of individual weapons.

The M41 Rifle Division (5 April 1941), with personnel reduced to 14,483, had a reorganized HQ reconnaissance battalion with motor rifle, light tank and armoured car companies, an additional chemical company, and artillery regiments expanded to five 3-battery battalions. This organization proved too ambitious given the Red Army's massive and rapid expansion, so a new 10,859-strong M41 Rifle Division was introduced from 24 July 1941. This had only five battalions of HQ Troops (AA, AT, engineer, signals and medical) and two HQ Troops companies (motorized reconnaissance, and supply), and a single field artillery regiment with two 3-battery battalions. The third-type M41 Rifle Division (December 1941) will be discussed in the second volume of this study.

The Red Army also established 19 Mountain Rifle divisions, recruiting heavily in the Transcaucasian Military District; these were numbered 9, 20, 28, 30, 47, 58, 63, 68, 76, 77, 79, 83, 96, 138, 173, 192, 194, 242 and 302. Uniquely, an M40 Mountain Rifle Division (*Gornostrelkovaya Diviziya*) of August 1940 had four 5-company mountain regiments, omitting the intermediate battalion echelon. The troops, though recruited from mountainous regions and given horse and mule supply transport, received no specific mountain training; unlike the élite

German mountain divisions, they did not distinguish themselves in battle.

Divisions: Motorized and Tank

Twenty-eight Motorized divisions, each 11,200 strong, were formed from 1939 for the mechanized corps: these were numbered 1st Moscow Proletarian, 15, 36, 44, 57, 69, 81, 82, 95, 101, 103, 106, 109, 139, 163, 198, 202, 204, 205, 208–210, 213, 216, 219, 220, 236 and 266. Two divisions were later redesignated Guards Motorized Divisions: 1st (1st Moscow Proletarian) and 2nd (107th).

An M41 Motorized Division (*Motorizovannaya Diviziya*) had an HQ; four battalions of HQ Troops (recce, AT, AA and engineer); plus a five-battalion light tank regiment, an artillery regiment with three 3-battery battalions, and two 3-battalion motor rifle regiments. They were converted to standard rifle divisions following the deactivation of the mechanized corps from 15 July 1941.

Fifty-seven Tank divisions (numbered 2–56, 58, 60) were allocated to mechanized corps, and five more (1, 57, 59, 61, 69) fought as independent units. An 11,343-strong M41 Tank Division (*Tankovaya Diviziya*) complemented the motorized division, with an HQ; four battalions of HQ Troops (recce, AT, engineer, and signals); plus two 3-battalion tank regiments, a motor rifle regiment, and a two-battalion artillery regiment. Following the disbandment of the mechanized corps in July 1941 the remaining units were reorganized into ten independent Tank divisions (numbered 101, 102, 104, 105, 107–112), each with a recce and a light AA battalion, two 3-battalion tank regiments, and one each motor rifle and artillery regiments.

Divisions: Cavalry and Cossack

Twenty-four Cavalry divisions (numbered in the 1-44 series) had been formed by May 1940, but by June 1941 disbandments had left only nine remaining (3, 4, 6, 8, 24, 25, 32, 36 and 44). An M39 Cavalry Division (*Kavaleriyskaya Diviziya*) had an HQ; seven company-sized squadrons of HQ Troops (AA, AT, engineer, signals, supply, medical, and chemical); plus a mechanized regiment with a three-company tank battalion and a mechanized battalion (armoured car squadron, motor rifle company, artillery battery); a horse artillery regiment with two 3-battery battalions; and four mounted cavalry regiments, each with a machine-gun squadron and five mounted squadrons.

The 9,240-strong M40 Cavalry Division expanded the AA squadron to a battalion, and the tank and mechanized battalions were reorganized as a tank regiment. The M41 Cavalry Division was introduced on 6 July 1941 to replace the disbanded mechanized corps as a mobile formation. It had an HQ; HQ Troops without AA or AT units; plus a single tank squadron, a horse artillery battalion, and only three mounted cavalry regiments, each with an MG squadron and four mounted squadrons. The Cavalry branch expanded once again, and by December 1941 had formed 77 Cavalry divisions: 3–4, 6–8, 10, 11, 19, 23–32, 34–36, 38, 40, 43, 44, 46, 47, 49–56, 59–62, 64, 66, 68, 70, 72–74, 76–82, 84–87, 91, 94, and 97–114. Six divisions were redesignated Guards Cavalry Divisions: 1st (formerly 5th), 2nd (9th), 3rd (50th), 4th (53rd), 5th (2nd) and 6th (14th).

Marshal Tuchachevsky had relaxed the official disapproval of the traditional warrior-farmer caste of Cossacks living in southern Russia, previously condemned as Tsarist counter-revolutionaries. From 23 April 1936, 13 Don, Kuban and Terek Cossack divisions were recruited, but only three (12, 13, 63) still existed by December 1941.

The 11th Cavalry Division was a North Caucasian formation dating from at least 4 June 1926, and joined by the Independent Mountain Cavalry Brigade on 27 May 1936. By June 1941 there were four mountain cavalry divisions (17, 18, 20, 21); three more were then added (1, 39, 83), but by December 1941 only 39th Division remained. A Mountain Cavalry Division (*Gornokavaleriyskaya Diviziya*) had three mounted cavalry regiments, a tank squadron, but no mechanized regiment. Six 'Light Cavalry' divisions were formed in July 1941 (including 41, 57, 75), each with three mounted regiments and an artillery battalion, but their low firepower proved a major handicap, and five had been disbanded by December 1941.

SUMMARY OF LAND FORCES CAMPAIGNS

The 'Re-occupation Campaign', 1939–40

Stalin, fearful of military attack from a hostile Europe, was determined to annex six former Imperial Russian territories on the western borders that had been independent since the Russian Civil War, in order to push the vulnerable western frontier well away from Moscow, Leningrad and the Russian heartland. These territories were Finland, Estonia, Latvia, Lithuania, eastern Poland (western Byelorussia and Ukraine), and Rumanian Bessarabia. Stalin secured Hitler's compliance through the Nazi-Soviet Non-Aggression Pact of 23 August 1939. When Soviet occupation was achieved, perhaps half a million military personnel, government officials and other leading citizens of these territories were subject to imprisonment, deportation to Siberia and execution. The Soviet losses noted below are totals of land, air and naval personnel killed, missing, taken prisoner (and shot by the NKVD for alleged cowardice) during the four phases of this campaign:

Eastern Poland, 17–26 October 1939 As German forces advanced through western Poland, the Byelorussian and Ukrainian Fronts (450,000 men) occupied eastern Poland up to the Narev, Vistula and San rivers, incorporating the territory into Byelorussian SSR and Ukrainian SSR. (Losses 1,315.)

Baltic states, 28 September 1939–14 June 1940 Stalin pressurized Estonia, Latvia and Lithuania to accept garrisons of 75,000 Red Army troops during September–October 1939, followed by an almost peaceful occupation on 14 June 1940, with no combat losses.

Finland, 30 November 1939–13 March 1940 Finland refused to accept territorial demands and a Red Army garrison. Six North-Western Front armies from Leningrad Military District (425,640 men, later 750,578) attacked Finland across the

Viipuri, Karelian Isthmus, at the end of the Winter War in March 1940: two Red Army cameramen pose cheerfully in front of Armoured Train No.16. Both wear the M27 *budyonovka* field cap, the man on the left with a quilted khaki *telogreika;* his comrade is probably an officer cadet, wearing an officer's belt and greatcoat but with plain collar patches. (Tshakov Collection)

The Soviet Union and Nazi Germany were uneasy 'allies' during the life of their cynical Non-Aggression Pact, 23 August 1939–21 June 1941. Here, at a victory parade in Warsaw on 22 September 1939 after their joint occupation of Poland, Red Army officers in black leather jackets gaze uncomfortably while a German Army band studiously ignores them. (Tshakov Collection)

Karelian Isthmus and from Soviet Karelia in the 'Winter War'. The greatly outnumbered Finnish forces, with only some 70,000 men, inflicted heavy punishment that exposed Soviet military weaknesses, but were finally forced to accept an armistice, with the loss of Finland's second city Viipuri (now Vyborg) and extensive border areas. (Losses 85,000, against Finnish losses of *c*.25,000 killed.)[3]

Bessarabia and Northern Bukovina, 28 June–4 July 1940 Since Rumania's ally France was defeated by Germany on 25 June 1940, the government did not resist the Red Army Southern Front's occupation of Bessarabia – redesignated the Moldavian SSR – and annexation of Northern Bukovina (which had never been Russian) to Ukrainian SSR.

The 'Great Patriotic War'

Both Stalin and Hitler regarded the Nazi-Soviet Non-Agression Pact cynically as a temporary expedient, but Stalin was still taken by surprise when Hitler launched Operation 'Barbarossa' – the invasion of the USSR on 22 June 1941 by 4.5 million German, Finnish, Rumanian, Hungarian and Slovak troops. The resulting four-year war was the greatest, most costly and probably the most brutal conflict of modern history, driven by the equally merciless ideologies of Communism and National Socialism in the service of two totalitarian regimes; this confrontation was, on the Nazi side, openly racial, proclaiming the 'sub-human' status of the Slavic peoples. The first six months saw 13 identifiably separate campaigns, with the huge but utterly outclassed Red Army in full retreat, before it managed to hold ground and begin local counter-attacks from mid-November 1941. Soviet military losses alone reached the staggering figure of 3,131,800 men during these campaigns:

Baltic states, 22 June–27 July 1941 North-Western Front retreated 300 miles through Lithuania, Latvia and Estonia before German Army Group North, losing 75,200 men.

Byelorussia, 22 June–9 July 1941 Western Front retreated 400 miles, abandoning most of Byelorussia to Army Group Centre, losing 341,000 men but leaving pockets of resistance in Brest-Litovsk, Bialystok and Minsk.

---

3 See Osprey Elite 141: *Finland at War 1939–45.*

Western Ukraine, 22 June–6 July 1941 South-Western and Southern Fronts retreated 200 miles, allowing Army Group Centre to occupy western Ukraine west of Kiev, and losing 172,300 men.

Arctic and Karelia, 29 June–10 October 1941 Northern Front – later divided into Karelian and Leningrad Fronts – retreated up to 100 miles through Soviet Karelia and the Karelian Isthmus before advancing Finnish and German forces, losing 67,200 men.

Kiev, 7 July–26 September 1941 South-Western, Southern and Central Fronts unsuccessfully defended Kiev from Army Group South, and retreated 400 miles across central Ukraine, losing 616,000 men – easily the greatest defeat of World War II.

Leningrad, 28 July–30 September 1941 Northern, North-Western and Leningrad Fronts retreated 200 miles to the gates of Leningrad before Army Group North, losing 214,000 men.

Smolensk, 10 July–10 September 1941 Western, Central, Reserve and Bryansk Fronts unsuccessfully defended Smolensk from Army Group Centre, retreating 180 miles and losing 486,000 men.

Donbass-Rostov, 29 September–16 November 1941 South-Western and Southern Fronts retreated 200 miles before Army Group South, abandoning the industrial Donbass region and eastern Ukraine but holding Rostov. Losses were 143,300 men.

Moscow, 30 September–5 December 1941 Western, Reserve, Kalinin and Bryansk Fronts retreated 200 miles to the outskirts of Moscow before Army Group Centre's Operation 'Typhoon' (beginning 2 October), losing 514,300 men.

Tikhvin, 10 November–30 December 1941 North-Western, Leningrad and Volkhov Fronts counter-attacked, advancing 80 miles and driving a wedge between Army Groups North and Centre, thus preventing the encirclement of Leningrad and Moscow, at a cost of 17,900 men.

Rostov, 17 November–2 December 1941 Southern Front relieved Rostov and prevented further advances by Army Group South, losing 315,300 men.

Moscow, 5 December 1941–7 January 1942 Western, South-Western, Kalinin and Bryansk Fronts counter-attacked 150 miles, pushing Army Group Centre away from Moscow, at a cost of 139,600 men.

Kerch-Feodosia, 25 December 1941–2 January 1942 In an amphibious operation, Transcaucasian (later Caucasus) Front retook the Kerch peninsula, blocking Army Group South's advance into the Caucasus, but losing 32,400 men.

LAND FORCES UNIFORMS

3 December 1935–12 July 1940[4]

The Red Army represented a clean break with previous 'traditionalist' Russian armies, to the extent of replacing officer rank titles with 'positional' titles indicating levels of command. The uniforms introduced from 16 January 1919 had cuff rank insignia instead of shoulder boards, and branch-of-service was indicated by sleeve badges instead of coloured

---

4 The separation of this subject into three volumes by date cannot be pedantically consistent, for reasons of relative space. The changes introduced from 13 July 1940 will be covered in the second volume.

collar patches. This system was later modernized during the 'Tukhachevsky period'.

The Red Army Dress Regulations of 17 December 1936 (see Table 2) prescribed service, guard duty and field uniforms, in winter and summer versions, for all ranks, with officers, officer cadets and re-enlisted NCOs permitted undress versions of the service uniforms. There was no ceremonial uniform. All mentioned items of the M35 khaki uniform (of a slightly greenish brown) were introduced from 3 December 1935. The M35 button was brass with a star, hammer and sickle, and the retained standard cap badge (introduced 11 July 1922) was a red metal star edged yellow, bearing a yellow hammer and sickle.

Summer 1941: a German NCO (right) herds Red Army soldiers taken prisoner during the Axis advances past a blazing BT-7 light tank – and into a desperately uncertain future. The Soviet soldiers wear M35 uniforms and M36 helmets. (Nik Cornish Collection)

Headgear

The peaked (visored) cloth field cap with ear-flaps introduced 8 April 1919 was nicknamed the *budyonovka* after Semyon Budyonny, and was modelled on the 'spired' shape of a 12th-century Kievan Rus knight's helmet. The model introduced 3 September 1927 was mid-grey for enlisted ranks, dark grey for officers, with an M22 cap badge on a large branch-colour cloth star; this was the standard winter service and field headgear. The M28 khaki-painted steel helmet with a large metal M22 badge was derived from the French M15 Adrian helmet; the khaki-painted M36 *Schvartz* helmet, with an applied 'comb' and often with a large red-painted outline of the cap badge, saw limited issue. The M35 khaki woollen peaked service cap had a branch-colour band with M22 badge, branch-colour piping to the crown seam and upper band edge, and black patent leather chin strap and peak. The optional white summer service cap had a white band, cloth chin strap and peak. The M35 *pilotka* khaki cotton sidecap had an M22 badge on a small branch-colour cloth star, and for officers branch-colour crown and flap piping. In cold weather officers wore the M31 'Finnish' fleece cap introduced 31 January 1931 – a khaki 'pillbox' with dark grey or brown sheepskin front- and side-flaps and an M22 badge. It and the *budyonovka* were both superseded from 5 July 1940 by the *ushanka* flapped cap, a grey woollen pillbox with a grey fleece fold-up peak bearing the M22 badge, and fold-up fleece ear flaps. The M38 light khaki cotton *panama* brimmed field hat, with a cloth chin strap and the M22 badge on a large branch-colour cloth star, was introduced 10 March 1938 for troops in Central Asia, North Caucasian and Transcaucasian military districts and Crimea.

Tunics and field shirts

The officers' M35 khaki cloth or worsted closed-collar service tunic, nicknamed the *French* after the British Field-Marshal Sir John French, had six front buttons, pleated patch breast pockets with buttoned scalloped flaps, internal waist pockets with plain scalloped flaps, branch-colour piping on the collar and cuffs, and collar and cuff rank insignia. A plain white summer tunic was optional. The M35 khaki cotton (in summer, light khaki) field shirt was the traditional Russian *gymnastiorka* with a fold-down collar, buttons concealed by a fly front, two-button shirt cuffs, and patch breast pockets with scalloped buttoned flaps. Officers had branch-colour collar and cuff piping; in summer they could wear a white unpiped version. In cold weather personnel wore a khaki quilted *telogreika* overjacket with four black horn buttons and two patch waist pockets, with either M31 fold-down or M38 buttoned stand-up collars, worn with quilted *vatnie sharovari* overtrousers. For snow camouflage a white cotton hooded coat or hooded smock and trousers were worn.

Overcoats

The officers' M35 dark grey double-breasted greatcoat had two rows of four buttons, an open or closed collar, straight stitched cuffs, internal diagonal waist pockets with flaps, and a buttoned rear half-belt. Collar

Table 2: Red Army Orders of Dress, 17 December 1936–12 July 1940

Uniform	Officers (1) (2) (4)	Non-Commissioned Officers and Men (3)
Winter Service Uniform (daily duties and exercises in formation with troops)	M27 dark grey peaked field cap; M35 dark grey closed-collar greatcoat; M35 khaki service tunic or M35 khaki field shirt; M35 coloured breeches; riding boots; M35 service belt and crossbrace; gloves.	M27 mid-grey peaked field cap; M35 mid-grey closed-collar greatcoat; M35 khaki field shirt; M35 khaki trousers; marching boots; M35/40 enlisted belt (6); gloves.
Winter Service Uniform (undress) (meetings off duty, classes, leave and exercises not in formation with troops)	M27 dark grey peaked field cap or M35 khaki peaked service cap or M31 fur cap; M35 dark grey open-collar greatcoat or M31 lined cloth coat or fur-collared leather coat; M35 khaki service tunic; M35 khaki trousers; black shoes or felt boots; M35 service belt and crossbrace optional; gloves; scarf.	As above. Re-enlisted NCOs wore the M31 Finnish cap or M35 khaki peaked service cap, fur-lined greatcoat or fur-collared leather coat or jacket, and felt boots.
Summer Service Uniform (daily duties and exercises in formation with troops)	M35 khaki peaked service cap or M35 khaki sidecap; M35 dark grey open-collar greatcoat; M35 light khaki summer field shirt; M35 coloured breeches; riding boots; M35 service belt and crossbrace.	M35 peaked service cap or M35 khaki sidecap; M35 light khaki summer field shirt; M35 light khaki summer trousers; marching boots; M35/40 enlisted belt (6).
Summer Service Uniform (undress) (meetings off duty, classes, leave and exercises not in formation with troops)	M35 khaki or M35 white peaked service cap; M35 dark grey open-collar greatcoat or leather coat or leather jacket or M31 raincoat; M35 khaki or M35 white service tunic or M35 white field shirt; M35 coloured breeches or M35 white breeches with riding boots or M35 khaki trousers or M35 white trousers with black or white shoes; M35 service belt and crossbrace optional; gloves.	As above.
Winter and Summer Guard Duty Uniform (patrols, standing guard, parades, reporting to a superior).	M27 dark grey peaked field cap or M35 khaki peaked service cap or M35 khaki sidecap; M35 dark grey closed-collar greatcoat; M35 khaki field shirt; M35 coloured breeches; riding boots; felt boots; M35 service belt and crossbrace and M32/33/38 holster with field shirt; M32 field belt, M35/38 supporting braces, M32/33/38 holster with greatcoat; gloves.	M27 mid-grey peaked field cap; M35 mid-grey closed-collar greatcoat; M35 khaki field shirt; M35 khaki trousers; marching boots; felt boots; M35/40 enlisted belt (6); one brown M17/37 ammo pouch; gloves.
Winter and Summer Field Uniform (marches, manoeuvres, field-exercises, active service)	M27 dark grey peaked field cap, M35 khaki sidecap or M28/36 helmet; M35 dark grey closed-collar greatcoat; M35 light khaki field shirt; M31/38 quilted overjacket; white camouflage coat or overjacket; M35 khaki breeches; white camouflage trousers; riding boots; winter boots; felt boots; M32 field belt, M35/38 supporting braces; binocular case, M32/33/38 holster; M35/37/38 dispatch-case, water bottle and SM-1 gasmask case.	M27 mid-grey peaked field cap or M28/36 helmet; M35 khaki sidecap or M38 *panama* hat; M35 light khaki summer field shirt; M31/38 quilted overjacket; white camouflage coat or overjacket; M35 khaki trousers; white camouflage trousers; marching boots; felt boots; M35/38 field belt; M38 supporting braces; two M17/37 ammo pouches; M38/39 backpack; shelter-half; entrenching tool, waterbottle; mess-kit and SM-1 gasmask case; field bag; bayonet.

Notes:
(1) Armoured Troops officers wore a steel-grey M27 peaked field cap, M35 peaked service cap, M35 sidecap, M35 officers' greatcoat, M35 open-collar service tunic, M35 field shirt, M35 breeches and M35 trousers with red piping.
(2) Air Force officers wore a dark blue M35 peaked field cap, M35 peaked service cap, M35 sidecap, M35 officers' greatcoat, M35 open-collar service tunic, M35 field shirt, M35 breeches and M35 trousers with light blue piping.
(3) Air Force NCOs and men wore a dark blue M35 peaked field cap and M35 sidecap and M35 breeches.
(4) Cadets wore officers' uniform with some enlisted uniform items.
(5) A *Starshina* wore an M32/38 officers' belt and crossbrace.
(6) Cadets wore a special leather belt.

and cuff rank insignia were worn, with branch-colour cuff and collar piping for junior general officers (*kombrig – komkor*), also front edge piping for senior generals (*komandarm 2-go ranga – marshal Sovetskogo Soyuza*). Officers could also wear the khaki cloth double-breasted M31 *bekesha* coat, introduced 31 January 1931, with a wide merino-wool collar, fur, fleece or padded lining, and three concealed front buttons; or a black or brown leather double-breasted greatcoat with two rows of four black buttons, buttoned cuff-tabs, and two internal waist pockets with square flaps. The enlisted ranks' M35 plain mid-grey double-breasted greatcoat had one row of front buttons concealed by a fly front, straight stitched cuffs, and internal waist pockets without flaps.

Legwear and footwear

For service dress, officers wore M35 navy-blue woollen riding breeches piped in branch colour, with black leather riding boots (spurred for mounted officers). For undress they wore M35 khaki woollen trousers with branch-colour seam piping, and black leather shoes, and in summer M35 plain white cloth trousers were permitted. In the field, M35 plain khaki (in summer, light khaki) cotton breeches were worn. In cold weather white felt *valenki* boots with brown or black rubber soles and trim were available. For service and field uniforms enlisted men wore plain khaki (in summer, light khaki) cloth *sharovari* trousers, full-cut in the thigh, tapered to the knee and tucked into black leather marching boots, or khaki cloth puttees and brown leather ankle-boots, and in extreme cold they received plain grey felt *valenki*.

Equipment

In service dress, officers wore the M35 brown leather belt with a star buckle and right shoulder crossbrace, with brass fittings. Officers' M32 undress field equipment introduced 19 September 1932 comprised a brown leather belt and left shoulder crossbrace, with a double-claw buckle and white metal fittings, and a brown leather holster on the right hip. M32 officers' field equipment comprised the belt, two shoulder braces, holster, and a brown leather binocular case on the right front hip; M35 or M37 brown leather mapcase on the left hip, or slung from the right shoulder on a narrow strap; SM-1 gasmask in a light grey canvas bag, on a broad sling to the left hip; and a tin waterbottle in a light grey cloth pouch behind the left hip. The M38 officers' field equipment had supporting braces, holster and mapcase in greenish-grey canvas with brown leather reinforcements.

With service uniform, NCOs and men wore the M35 brown leather enlisted ranks' belt with a white metal single-claw buckle, but the *starshina* wore an officer-quality enlisted belt with a right shoulder brace. Enlisted field equipment was based on the M35 brown leather belt, or M38 greyish-green canvas field belt with leather reinforcements. This supported two 20-round brown leather M17 or M37 rifle ammunition pouches on the front; often the bayonet scabbard on the left front,

Summer 1941: three Red Army officers and an NCO in khaki M35 field uniforms, with *pilotka* sidecaps and field shirts. (Left) unidentified; (second left) a *mladshiy leytenant*; (second right) a *mayor*, displaying the M40 infantry branch badge on his collar patches, and the red enamel Order of the Red Star; and (right), an *otdelyonniy komandir* of artillery. (Nik Cornish Collection)

Two artillerymen in M40 enlisted ranks' field uniform, with M40 Ssh-39 steel helmets. Both have black M40 collar patches piped red, with branch badges; under magnification, those of the *serzhant* (left) show the red central stripe and three brass triangles of that rank. Both carry M1891/30 rifles with fixed bayonets, and SM-1 gasmask bags slung from their right shoulders. (Tshakov Collection).

and a bag for rations and mess kit at the rear centre; and an entrenching tool and a tin waterbottle in a grey cloth cover on the right hip. M38 light grey or brown canvas straps supported the M38 light grey or olive-brown canvas knapsack or the simpler M39 bag. An olive-brown canvas *plashch-palatka* hooded cape/shelter-half was carried either inside the M38 knapsack, strapped around it, around the torso in a roll with the greatcoat, or tied to the back of the belt. The SM-1 gasmask in its bag was carried slung from the right shoulder, and sometimes a haversack from the left; in practice, from 1941 the mask was often discarded and its bag used as a general-purpose haversack.

Branch-specific uniforms

Staff and officer students attending the Red Army **General Staff Academy** wore from 27 October 1936 a khaki service tunic and a dark-grey greatcoat with a black velvet collar, while the M36 navy-blue service breeches and M36 khaki service trousers had white piping flanked by two 1.5cm crimson stripes.

As an élite branch, **armoured troops** officers were issued M35 uniforms in light 'steel-grey'. This included a *budyonovka* field cap; peaked service cap; *pilotka* sidecap; M38 field hat; and an open-collar four-button service tunic, with two rear cuff buttons, pleated patch breast pockets with buttoned scalloped flaps, internal waist pockets with scalloped flaps, and red piping on the collar and cuffs, worn with a white shirt and black tie. Grey cloth winter and light cotton summer field shirts, woollen service trousers, and cloth winter and light cotton summer breeches completed the uniform.

In the field, armoured officers wore the M29 black leather jacket with two rows of five buttons and internal waist pockets with square flaps, and black leather breeches; or a dark blue 'moleskin' jacket with two rows of five buttons, buttoned cuff tabs and a patch right breast pocket with a square buttoned flap, with matching breeches. Tank and motor vehicle crews wore the M33 black leather padded helmet, and the M35 blue cloth tank overall with a cloth belt, fly front, two-button shirt cuffs, an internal left breast pocket with a squared buttoned flap, and a large buttoned patch pocket on the right thigh.

Mounted cavalry and field artillery officers wore a longer dark grey greatcoat from 17 December 1935. Cavalry officers wore royal-blue riding breeches. Cavalry officers and field artillery battery commanders carried silver-mounted officer-pattern M26 sabres with brown leather sword knot and scabbard, and NCOs and men the brass-mounted enlisted version.

Terek, Kuban and Don **Cossack** units were issued traditional ceremonial and service uniforms from 23 April 1936. In service uniform, Terek Cossacks wore a 10–11cm high black lambskin *kubanka* cap, with an M22 badge, and a double black (officers, gold) braid cross on the light blue cloth crown. Their light blue fitted *beshmet* high-collar tunic bore cavalry collar patches; officers had light blue braid edged in gold on the collar and front. The baggy dark blue *sharovari* trousers were piped light blue, and worn over black leather riding boots. The M32 belt and shoulder brace supported a Cossack-pattern *shashka* sabre with brown leather sword knot. Ceremonial uniform added a light blue, black-fringed *bashlyk* hood, and a light grey open-necked *cherkeska* frock-coat with a row of nine cartridge tubes on each breast; a black felt *burka* cloak with yoked shoulders; and a silver-mounted *kindjal* dagger in a silver-and-black scabbard suspended from a narrow black cross belt to the left hip, or a sabre suspended from a brown leather cross belt. Kuban Cossacks wore a red cap crown, tunic, trouser-piping and hood, and a dark blue frock-coat. Don Cossacks had a taller, floppier black lambskin *papachka* cap with a red cloth crown; a dark blue *kazazin* high-collar tunic with red piping on the collar and pointed cuffs; 4cm red trouser-stripes; and a light grey hood, but no frock-coat.

The Independent Caucasian **Mountain Cavalry** Brigade's ceremonial uniform introduced 27 May 1936 had a brown lambskin *kubanka* cap with a red crown; a red Caucasian high-collar satin shirt with cavalry collar patches, black cord collar- and front-piping (gold for officers), black cord buttons, and black cord piping on the edges of the patch pockets and square pocket flaps; dark blue cavalry trousers piped red; dark brown leather riding boots; a red hood; and a black frock-coat. Conventional cavalry service uniform was worn with the lambskin cap and a khaki Caucasian shirt.

Branch distinctions

The branch distinctions of the *marshal Sovetskogo Soyuza*, RKKA General Staff Academy, and the 21 Land Forces branches were identified by a combination of the following features (see Table 3):

Six **facing colours** (red, crimson, blue, black, light blue and dark green), worn on the band of the officers' M35 service cap, the M35 greatcoat collar patches, and M35 tunic and field shirt collar patches.

Seven **piping colours** (red, white, crimson, black, blue, royal-blue and light blue), worn on the crown and upper band edge of the officers' M35 service cap; the collar and cuffs of the officers' M35 service tunic and field shirt; the collar patches of the M35 political officers' tunic, and of the M35 enlisted field shirt; the collar, cuffs and front of the M35 greatcoat for *marshal Sovetskogo Soyuza – komandarm 2-go ranga*, and collar and cuffs of the M35 greatcoat for *komkor – kombrig*; M35 greatcoat collar patches, and M35 officers' service breeches and trousers.

Nineteen brass (Veterinary, white metal) **branch badges**, introduced 10 March 1936 to replace the 23 white metal badges introduced 20 June 1924.

Infantry, as the core combat arm, initially had no branch badge, but the brass crossed rifles on a white-and-brass target was introduced in 1940 for ranks below general officer. The Supply and Administration Service had not previously worn a branch badge before the March 1936 regulation. Technical and Legal officers and Bandmasters wore branch badges on the collar patches of the combat arm to which they were attached.

October 1941: a *starshiy leytenant* deputy company commander photographed beside an obsolete M28 MS light tank; his 20 Years' Service Medal suggests that he is a commissioned former NCO. His officers' M35 field shirt has khaki subdued-pattern collar patches with infantry branch badges; the cuff chevrons were ordered removed from 1 August 1941. Note the *plashch-palatka* shelter-half worn as a rain cape, the mapcase with magnifying glass, and the PPD-40 sub-machine gun.

Political officers wore the crimson, blue or black collar patches, with the black, red or royal-blue piping, of the combat arm to which they were assigned. With the exception of the *zamestitel' politruka* they displayed no branch badge, making it impossible to distinguish between those in armoured, artillery or technical troops units.

Combat arms rank insignia

On 16 January 1919 the Red Army had adopted 'revolutionary' positional titles instead of traditional military titles, and cuff rank insignia (moved to collar patches, 20 June 1924) replacing the unpopular Imperial officers' *pogoni* shoulder boards.

New rank insignia and titles were introduced 3 December 1935 for combat arms (see Table 4). Officers were collectively styled

Table 3: Red Army Branch Distinctions, 10 March 1936–12 July 1940

Branch	Facing colour	Piping colour	Officer collar-patch piping	Brass branch badge on collar-patch
Marshal Sovetskogo Soyuza	Red	Red	Gold	None
RKKA General Staff Academy (27.10.1936 – 22.5.1940)	Crimson	White	Gold	None
Infantry	Crimson	Crimson (1)	Gold	None; Rifles & target (1940)
Cavalry	Blue	Blue (1)	Gold	Horseshoe on crossed sabres
Armoured Troops	Black (2)	Red	Gold	Tank (in pairs, gun facing right)
Motor Transport in all branches except Armour	Branch	Branch	Branch	Winged steering wheel, axle & wheels
Motorcycle units (1940)	Black (2)	Red	Gold	Motorcycle on cogwheel (in pairs)
Artillery	Black	Red	Gold	Crossed cannons
Artillery units in other branches	Branch	Branch	Gold	Crossed cannons
Engineers	Black	Royal blue	Gold	Crossed axes
Electrical Engineers	Black	Royal blue	Gold	Crossed axes on lightning bolts
Pontoon Engineers	Black	Royal blue	Gold	Crossed axes on sea-anchor
Railway Troops (10.3. – 30.8.1936)	Black	Royal blue	Gold	Crossed axe and anchor (pairs)
Military Transport Service and Railway Troops' officers (31.8.1936)	Black (2)	Royal blue	Gold	Red star on winged anchor, crossed hammer & wrench
Railway Troops' NCOs & Men (31.8.1936)	Black	Royal blue	–	Crossed hammer & wrench (pairs)
Construction Engineers	Black	Royal blue	Gold	Crossed pickaxe and spade (pairs)
Construction Engineers in other branches	Branch	Branch	Gold	Crossed pickaxe and spade (pairs)
Signals	Black	Royal blue	Gold	Red star on wings & lightning bolts
Signals units in other branches	Branch	Branch	Gold	Red star on wings & lightning bolts
Chemical Troops	Black	Black	Gold	Mask on crossed canisters
Chemical units in other branches	Branch	Branch	Gold	Mask on crossed canisters
Air Force and Paratroopers	Light blue (3)	Light blue (1)	Gold	Two-bladed winged propeller
Air Force Airfield Guards (1941)	Light blue (3)	Light blue (1)	Gold	Rifles & target
Supply & Administration Service	Dark green	Red	Red	Helmet, wrench, compasses, tyre & cogwheel
Medical Service	Dark green	Red	Red	Chalice & snake (pairs)
Veterinary Service	Dark green	Red	Red	White chalice & snake (pairs)
Technical Officers (combat arms)	Branch	Branch	Branch	Crossed hammer & wrench (pairs)
Legal Officers (combat arms)	Branch	Branch	Branch	Shield on crossed swords
Bandmasters (combat arms)	Branch	Branch	Branch	Lyre
Political Officers (combat arms)	Branch	Branch	–	None

Notes:
(1) Political Officer and enlisted collar-patch pipings were black.
(2) Black velvet facings for officers and officer cadets.
(3) The M36 peaked service cap had a dark blue band.

'commanders' and NCOs 'junior commanders'. General officers and NCOs retained pre-1935 positional titles, here listed in their common abbreviated form (e.g. *komdiv*, rather than *komandir divisii*), while field officers and subalterns now had military titles, and enlisted men were designated 'Red Army soldier'. The rank of *marshal Sovyetskogo Soyuza* was established on 22 September 1935, five general officers being promoted to marshal of the USSR on 20 November 1935: Budyonny, Blyukher, Tukhachevsky, Voroshilov and Yegorov. Three more were promoted marshal on 7 June 1940: Kulik, Shaposhnikov and Timoshenko.

The M35 rank insignia retained the M19 system of red diamonds, bars, squares and triangles, but these were now edged in gold (yellow metal). In addition, combat arm officers wore gold collar-patch piping, and gold embroidered stars and gold braid and red cloth chevrons (point down) above the cuffs. The M35 greatcoat collar patches were cloth rhomboids with piping, and a brass branch badge above the rank insignia; those of the M35 service tunic or field shirt were oblong cloth parallelograms with piping on three sides, and the branch badge behind the rank badges:

Marshal Sovetskogo Soyuza: 'Combined arms' red rhomboid collar patches piped gold, with a 6cm diameter (greatcoat) or 5cm (tunic/ field shirt) gold embroidered star; cuffs, 6cm (greatcoat) or 5cm (tunic/field shirt) gold star, above 3cm wide gold and 1.5cm medium red chevrons.

Komandarm 1-go ranga: Infantry-crimson collar patches piped gold, with 22mm gold star and 4 diamonds; cuffs, 6cm (greatcoat) or 5cm (tunic/ field-shirt) gold star above 3cm wide gold chevron.

Other general officers: Branch-colour (infantry, cavalry, armour, artillery only) collar patches piped gold, with branch badge and 4–1 diamonds; cuffs, 4–1x 1.5cm medium gold chevrons.

Field officers: Branch-colour collar patches piped gold, with branch badge and 3–1 bars; cuffs, 1.5cm medium red chevron with 0.5cm upper and lower gold edging, or 2–1x 1.5cm medium red chevrons. The rank of *podpolkovnik* (lieutenant-colonel) was announced 1 September 1939 but not introduced until 26 July 1940.

Subalterns: Branch-colour collar patches piped gold, with branch badge and 3–1 squares; cuffs, 3–1x 0.75cm narrow red chevrons.

NCOs: Branch-colour collar patch with branch-colour piping, branch badge, and 4–2 triangles.

Men: Branch-colour collar patch with branch-colour piping and branch badge.

Officer cadets (*kursanty*) wore mostly officers' uniform with NCOs' and men's rank insignia.

Services and Specialist Officers' rank insignia

Officers of the three Services (Supply and Administration, Medical, and Veterinary), and the four groups of Specialist Officers (Technical, Legal, Bandmasters, Political), were differentiated from the combat arms (see Table 5). The commissioned ranks were not designated as 'commanders'; they had military officials' rank titles, wore branch-colour collar-patch piping instead of gold, and did not wear cuff chevrons. Political officers

North-Western Front, 1941: the crew of a BT-7 tank from 2nd Tank Division pose for the camera. (From left to right) the driver-mechanic *Yefreytor* F. Lazarev, the gunner *Krasnoarmeyets* S. Kashekin, and the commander *Starshiy Serzhant* N. Ananyin. All wear M33 padded black leather helmets and dark blue 'moleskin' (brushed cotton) jackets, on which Lazarev has – against regulations – sewn greatcoat collar patches. All carry slung gasmask bags, and note the left-shoulder belt braces to support the weight of holstered revolvers at the right hip. (Tshakov Collection)

Autumn 1941: a Terek Cossack baggage train with escort. The Cossacks wear black lambskin *kubanka* caps, and black felt *burka* cloaks over M35 enlisted ranks' field shirts with cavalry collar patches. The escorts carry PPD-40 sub-machine guns. (Nik Cornish Collection)

wore special cuff insignia: the *Armeyskiy Komissar 1-go ranga* wore a 6cm (greatcoat) or 5cm (tunic) gold embroidered star, and subordinate ranks a 5.5cm red cloth star edged in red silk with a gold embroidered crossed hammer and sickle.

RED ARMY AIR FORCE

The air force was established as the Workers' and Peasants' Red Military Air Fleet (RKKVF) on 28 January 1918. Subsequently it underwent a series of cosmetic redesignations: to RKKA Air Force (*Vozdushnye Sily RKKA* – VS-RKKA) in 1935; RKKA Military Air Force (*Voenno-Vozdushnye Sily RKKA* – VVS-RKKA) in 1936; and Red Army Military Air Force (*Voenno-Vozdushnye Sily Krasnoy Armii* – VVS-KA) in September 1939. Russian sources refer to it simply as the VVS.

The VVS was a combat arm of the Red Army, commanded by the Head of the Air Force Main Directorate at the People's Commissariat for Defence: December 1937, *Komandarm 2-go ranga* Aleksandr Dmitrievich Loktionov; September 1939, *Komandarm 2-go ranga* Iakov Vladimirovich Smushkevich; 1940, *General-Leytenant Aviatsii* Pavel Vasilevich Rychagov; and April 1941, *General-Leytenant Aviatsii* Pavel Fedorovich Zhigarev. The VVS suffered particularly badly from Stalin's purges, and Loktionov, Smushkevich and Rychagov were all executed by the NKVD in 1941 for perceived military failures.

Air Force branches, 10 March 1936–31 December 1941

(1) Air Force. This comprised all elements except those listed below, including Fighter, Ground-Attack, Bomber and Night-Bomber Air Regiments; Airborne (Paratroop) Brigades; and Airfield Guard Battalions.

(2) Services. The Supply and Administration, Medical, and Veterinary Services were also available to the VVS.

(3) Specialist Officers. The VVS had their own Technical, Legal and Political Officers and Bandmasters.

1941: a *starshiy politruk* commissar attached to an artillery regiment, photographed in front of an M39 F-22 USV field gun. This political officer with a rank equivalent to captain wears the officers' M35 winter field uniform, with unpiped enlisted ranks' *pilotka*, and a greatcoat with his rank bar on black artillery collar patches piped red. He has an M32 officers' field belt and crossbrace, and a slung mapcase. (Imperial War Museum)

(continued on page 33)

ARMED FORCES COMMANDERS, 1939
1: *Marshal Sovetskogo Soyuza* Kliment Voroshilov
2: *Flagman Flota 2-go ranga* Nikolai Kuznetzov
3: *Komandarm 2-go ranga* Aleksandr Loktionov

A

KHALKIN-GOL, AND COSSACKS, 1939
1: *Komkor* G.K. Zhukov, 1st Army Group; Khalkin-Gol, Aug 1939
2: *Mladshiy Komvzvod*, 57th Rifle Div; Khalkin-Gol, June 1939
3: *Mladshiy Leytenant*, Kuban Cossacks; Northern Caucasus, 1939

2

3

1

B

EASTERN POLAND, SEPTEMBER 1939
1: *Polkovnik*, 22nd Tank Brigade, Byelorussian Front
2: Sniper, 81st Rifle Division, Ukrainian Front
3: *Starshina*, Red Banner Baltic Fleet

D

BALTIC STATES, 1940–41
1: *Leytenant*, Cavalry, 22nd Territorial Corps; Estonia, Sept 1940
2: *Starshina*, Armoured Troops, 5th Tank Div; Lithuania, June 1941
3: *Starshiy Mayor*, GUGB State Security; Tallinn, Aug 1941

E

BYELORUSSIA AND UKRAINE, 1941
1: *Marshal Sovetskogo Soyuza* S.K.Timoshenko, July 1941
2: *Kapitan*, NKVD Frontier Troops, June 1941
3: *Krasnoflotets*, Naval Infantry, Black Sea Fleet; Sevastopol, Nov 1941

F

WESTERN RUSSIA, 1941
1: *Yefreytor*, Artillery, 108th Rifle Div; Smolensk Pocket, July 1941
2: *Voenvrach 2-go ranga*, Medical Corps, 139th Rifle Div; Uman Pocket, Aug 1941
3: *Leytenant*, Northern Fleet; Rybachiy Peninsula, Nov 1941

G

MOSCOW, DECEMBER 1941
1: *Starshiy Leytenant*, Engineers, 173rd Mtn Rifle Div; Kashira
2: *Mladshiy Serzhant*, 11th Motorcycle Regt, Kalinin Front
3: Air Force pilot, Moscow Anti-Air Defence Zone

Organization of air units, April 1939–31 December 1941

In April 1939 the Air Division began to replace the Air Brigade (*Aviabrigada*) as the principal tactical flying formation. Between five and eight air divisions were allocated to each of the 13 existing Military Districts, the two Independent Red Banner Armies (1st, 2nd), and the three Special Purpose Air Armies (AON 1–3) formed from 1936 for strategic operations.

Unsatisfactory VVS performance during the Winter War against Finland led to a reorganization into four principal groupings. The AONs were disbanded from 29 April 1940, and that November were largely re-formed under the single designation Long Range Bomber Air Force (*Dal'no-bombardirovochnaya Aviatsiya* – DBA) with five Air Corps. In early 1941 the Anti-Air Defence (*Protivovozdushnaya Oborona* – PVO) formed PVO Zones, one per Military District, to co-ordinate fighter air divisions, anti-aircraft and searchlight batteries, and balloon barrage defences. The Frontal Aviation (*Frontovaya Aviatsiya*) supported the Army Fronts with 61 air divisions, while 95 Army Aviation (*Armeiskaya Aviatsiya*) corps squadrons carried out reconnaissance missions for the field armies. The Aeroflot Civil Air Fleet (GVF) had formed Air Detachments (*Aviaotryady*) in June 1940 to transport troops to the Baltic and Bessarabia, and in June 1941 these formed VVS Transport Air Regiments.

The highest tactical formation was the Air Corps (*Aviakorpus*), with two or three air divisions. In June 1941 there were 79 air divisions – about 40 per cent fighters, 30 per cent ground-attack, 20 per cent bombers, 7 per cent night bombers, and 3 per cent mixed – mostly bearing 200-series numbers. An Air Division (*Aviadiviziya*) contained four to six air regiments; a Fighter or Ground Attack Air Regiment (*Aviapolk*) comprised a two-aircraft HQ Flight (*Zveno*) and four 15-aircraft squadrons (squadron = *Aviaeskadril'ya*), totalling 62 aircraft. A Bomber Air Regiment also had 62 aircraft, divided into a two-aircraft HQ Flight and five 12-aircraft squadrons; but a Heavy Bomber Air Regiment had 40 aircraft in four 10-aircraft squadrons. In 1941 some VVS personnel formed infantry-style Airfield Guard Battalions.

Summary of Air Force operations, 17 July 1936–31 December 1941

About 1,000 VVS volunteers served with the Republican Air Force in the Spanish Civil War, 1936–39. Some 450 pilots of the Soviet Volunteer Group of the Chinese Nationalist Air Force flew against the Japanese, October 1937–April 1941; and aircraft of the 1st and 2nd Independent Red Banner Armies fought them over Khalkin-Gol in 1939. VVS units faced minimal opposition in Eastern Poland; nevertheless, the occupation force that entered the Baltic states on 28 September 1939, under former VVS commander Aleksandr Loktionov, contained a large air contingent – two air brigades plus nine more air regiments. The VVS absorbed the Estonian, Latvian and Lithuanian air forces after June 1940. Although facing a Finnish Air Force with only about 145 aircraft, during the Winter War the VVS units in 7th–9th and 13th–15th Armies lost 700–900 aircraft, mostly

Leytenant Yakov Ivanovich Antonov, made a Hero of the Soviet Union on 21 March 1940 for attacks on Finnish military airfields between 6 December 1939 and 19 February 1940. Antonov was a deputy squadron commander in 25th Fighter Air Regiment, with 7th Army. He wears the khaki M40 Air Force officers' service cap with light blue band and M37 badges, and a khaki M35 field shirt with light blue piping. As well as his Hero's gold star he displays the Orders of Lenin and the Red Banner. (Tshakov Collection)

bombers, and in often atrocious weather conditions Soviet fighters were unable to defeat the Finnish and foreign volunteer (mostly Swedish) pilots.

In June–July 1941 the Luftwaffe rapidly achieved air supremacy over the ill-prepared and poorly equipped VVS, which, in spite of individual bravery, had lost 7,500 aircraft by September 1941. The VVS reasserted itself from 30 September during the battle for Moscow, when aircraft of 6th PVO Air Corps, the Stavka Reserve Air Corps and Frontal Aviation fought desperately. Despite suffering huge losses, they achieved local air superiority in winter conditions, helping to halt the German advance in December 1941.

AIR FORCE UNIFORMS

3 December 1935–13 July 1940

The VVS had dark blue M35 service uniforms with light blue branch-colour facings and piping. Officers wore a dark blue *budyonovka* field cap, with an M22 badge on a large light blue star; a dark blue *pilotka* sidecap piped light blue, with an M22 badge also backed by a light blue star; a dark blue greatcoat; an Armoured Troops' pattern dark blue open-collar four-button tunic, with piping on the collar and pointed cuffs, and two rear cuff buttons; a dark blue *gymnastiorka* field shirt with piping; and dark blue riding breeches or service trousers, with seam piping. In field uniform, a khaki *gymnastiorka* and breeches were worn. A dark blue peaked service cap with a dark blue band, light blue piping, and an M22 badge was adopted in 1936; in 1937 new gold-embroidered cap insignia were introduced, comprising a star and wings on the front of the crown, above the M22 badge pinned to a disc in a laurel wreath.

Conscript NCOs and men wore khaki Red Army uniforms with light blue facings and piping, and a plain dark blue M35 *pilotka*. Officer-style crown and flap piping and cloth cap-badge backing was introduced for this from 9 June 1936; with field uniform a plain khaki *pilotka* was worn. Ex-Aeroflot personnel could wear VVS uniform with the Aeroflot gold-embroidered M36 cap badge – a winged propeller on a blue cockade edged gold in a laurel wreath, below a hammer and sickle. Cadets and re-enlisted NCOs (*starshina* and *mladshiy komzvzod*) wore many officers' uniform items, including the dark blue tunic, but without branch piping.

VVS issue flying clothing included fur-lined brown leather winter flying helmets, gauntlets or mittens; M33 unlined brown leather summer flying helmets and brown leather and suede gauntlets; goggles, and a black moleskin face mask. Khaki winter flight overalls had a large brown fur collar and lining, a front zipper concealed by a fly, and two large patch thigh pockets with square buttoned flaps; M35 blue summer flight overalls were identical to the tank overalls. Also worn were black or brown leather double-breasted fly-fronted overcoats with buttoned cuff tabs; dark blue double-breasted thigh-length coats with large brown fur collars and lining; fur-lined white felt *valenki* boots or black fur *unty* flying boots, both with brown or black rubber soles and trim.

Flying clothing, 1941: pilots posed as if listening attentively to an article in *Pravda* being read out by the *starshiy leytenant* commanding their Naval Aviation fighter squadron, equipped with the obsolete M39 Polikarpov I-153 *Chaika* ('Seagull'). They wear M33 brown leather unlined flying helmets and black leather coats; only one M24 pilot's qualification sleeve badge is visible. (Imperial War Museum)

Air Force insignia

The M36 branch badge was a brass winged two-blade propeller. Technical and legal officers and bandmasters wore light blue collar patches piped black with the appropriate brass badge, and political officers without a badge. The VVS used standard Red Army M35 rank titles, collar and cuff rank insignia (see Table 4). *Komandarm 1-go ranga* was the highest rank, and the only one not to wear the branch badge on the collar patches.

There were three types of flight qualification 'wings'; these were worn as a red cloth star on a large gold or silver embroidered badge on a dark blue cloth backing, centred on the left upper sleeve of the M35 dark blue tunic and service shirt and khaki field shirt. From 8 August 1924, pilots wore the red star on a gold two-blade propeller and silver crossed swords (blades downwards) with gold hilts, on silver wings; airship and balloon crews wore a red star on a silver anchor with a gold rope, on gold wings. From 6 November 1925, flight technicians wore a red star on a gold two-blade propeller and gold crossed hammer and wrench, on silver wings. These personnel also wore above their left breast pocket elaborate gilt, silver and enamel military school graduation badges, introduced 28 August 1936 and redesigned 31 October 1938.

AIRBORNE FORCES

The first Air Force parachute unit was formed in March 1931, followed by 3rd Airborne Brigade on 11 December 1932 – the world's first operational airborne unit. The Airborne Forces (*Vozdushno-Desantnye Voiska* – VDV) steadily expanded, and by 1940 comprised six brigades (numbered 201, 202, 204, 211, 212 and 214) and three regiments (1–3), allocated to various Military Districts.

From April 1941 the VDV expanded to five corps (1–5), attached to various Fronts and transported by obsolete Tupolev TB-3 bombers. An Airborne Corps (*Vozdushno-Desantnye Korpus*) comprised an HQ; HQ Troops including an air-landed light tank battalion; plus three airborne brigades. 1st Corps (with brigades numbered 1st, 204th, 211th) was with South-Western Front; 2 Corps (2–4), Central and South-Western Fronts; 3 Corps (5, 6, 212), Southern Front; 4 Corps (7, 8, 214), Western Special Front; 5 Corps (9, 10, 201), Baltic Special and North-Western Fronts. From April 1941 a 3,000-strong Airborne Brigade (*Vozdushno-Desantnye Brigada*) comprised a Brigade HQ; HQ Troops (signals, bicycle reconnaissance, mortar, AA machine-gun companies; artillery battalion); plus four 458-man parachute battalions. In October 1941 an engineer company replaced the mortar company, and brigade establishment was reduced to 2,557 men.

The VDV were used extensively both for combat jumps and fighting as infantry. The 212nd Brigade fought at Khalkin-Gol in 1939. Three brigades (201st, 204th, 214th) fought with 8th Rifle Corps in Finland north of Lake Ladoga from 13 February 1940, and some small groups jumped behind Finnish lines at Summa and Petsamo to cut communications. The 201st Brigade dropped at Izmail in Bessarabia on 30 June 1940, where they were joined by 204th and 211th Brigades.

From June 1941, German air superiority restricted combat jumps to small sabotage operations, thus forcing the five airborne corps to fight as infantry. 1st and 3rd Corps fought in Western Ukraine and Kiev until October 1941; 2nd Corps at Smolensk and Kiev until October 1941; 4th Corps in Byelorussia and Smolensk until August 1941; and 5th Corps

in the Baltic and Smolensk until September 1941. To replace the shattered corps, five more 10,000-strong airborne corps (6–10) were formed in October 1941.

The VDV wore standard Air Force uniforms and insignia. The M31 parachute qualification badge, worn above the left breast pocket, showed a red star above a white parachute in a blue quadrilateral, while the M33 badge included a paratrooper figure. For combat jumps paratroopers wore a khaki cloth flying helmet and a khaki version of the blue tank/flight overall, often adding collar patches against regulations.

Trainee Air Force paratroopers receive instruction on the PL-3M parachute. All wear khaki cloth flying helmets and a khaki version of the M35 dark blue tank and flying overalls; not even the instructor (centre) displays any insignia. (Imperial War Museum)

NAVY

Without overseas colonies, the Soviet Union only required a navy to defend the coastal flanks of the Red Army. The Workers' and Peasants' Red Fleet (*Raboche-Krest'yansky Krasny Flot* – RKKF), formed 11 February (28 January OS) 1918, was redesignated the Military Sea Fleet (*Voenno-Morski Flot* – VMF) in 1939. It was administered by the People's Commissariat for the Navy, which was made independent of the People's Commissariat for Defence on 30 December 1937. People's Commissars were Petr Aleksandrovich Smirnov, 1937; *Flagman Flota 1-go ranga* Mikhail Petrovich Frinovskiy, 8 September 1938; and *Flagman Flota 2-go ranga* Nikolai Gerasimovich Kuznetzov, 28 April 1939. The Navy Commander-in-Chief, *Flagman Flota 1-go ranga* Mikhail Mitrovanich Viktorov, reported to Kuznetzov. The 34-year-old Kuznetzov was a consummate professional and an independent thinker, who managed to defend naval interests while avoiding Stalin's purges.

Naval branches, 10 March 1936–31 December 1941
(1) Seamen's. Four fleets and ten flotillas; naval infantry and rifle brigades.
(2) Coastal Defence. Coastal artillery regiments; naval railway artillery brigades and independent batteries; anti-aircraft artillery regiments and independent battalions.
(3) Naval Aviation (VVS-RKKF, then VVS-VMF). Formed 1 May 1935, and commanded from 1939 by *Flagman 2-go ranga* Semyon Fedorovich Zhavoronkov. This comprised fighter, torpedo, ground-attack, bomber, and mixed air divisions and air regiments attached to the fleets, with 2,581 aircraft in June 1941.
(4) Services. Supply and Administration Service; Medical Service.
(5) Specialist Officers. Technical Officers, including mechanical, electrical, artillery, mine and signals engineers, and naval architects; Legal Officers; and Political Officers.

Naval organization, April 1939–31 December 1941
The VMF was divided into sea-going fleets, lake flotillas with major vessels, and river flotillas with river monitors:

Northern Fleet. The smallest fleet, responsible for the Atlantic and Arctic Oceans and Barents and Norwegian Seas, with 50 vessels.
Red Banner Baltic Fleet, with 197 vessels.
Black Sea Fleet, with 196 vessels.
Pacific Fleet, with 297 vessels.
Lake Flotillas: Azov, Caspian, Kamchatka, Ladoga, and White Sea.
River Flotillas: Red Banner Amur, Danube, Dneproptrovsk, Pina, and Volga.

On 22 June 1941 the Navy totalled 740 major vessels: 3 battleships, 7 cruisers, 7 flotilla-leaders (small cruisers), 47 destroyers, 210 submarines, 22 guardships (protecting ports), 18 minelayers, 80 minesweepers, 269 torpedo-boats, and 77 submarine-chasers. Ships could be grouped into numbered brigades, subdivided into battalions (battalion = *divizion*).

Summary of naval operations

VMF volunteers fought for the Republican Navy in the Spanish Civil War, 1936–39. In the Winter War, 1939–40, the Baltic Fleet supported 7th Army's attack on the Karelian Isthmus, occupied Finland's Baltic islands, shelled coastal forts, and transported troops. Meanwhile the Northern Fleet secured the coast of Murmansk and supported 14th Army's landing at Petsamo, and the Ladoga Flotilla transported troops across Lake Ladoga. During the occupation of the Baltic states the Baltic Fleet gained several important Estonian, Latvian and Lithuanian ports.

Following the Axis invasion, the Northern Fleet and White Sea Flotilla defended Murmansk, and fought in the Arctic and Karelia 29 June–10 October 1941. The Baltic Fleet suffered huge losses while supporting land forces retreating through the Baltic states, 22 June–9 July 1941, and helped defend Leningrad, 10 July–30 September 1941. The Pina Flotilla supported the Western Front in Byelorussia, 22 June–9 July 1941, defended Smolensk 10 July–10 September 1941, and Kiev, 7 July–26 September 1941. The Azov Flotilla supported the Southern Front in the Donbass-Rostov operations of 29 September–16 November 1941, and, with the Black Sea Fleet, helped the Caucasus Front retake the Kerch Peninsula, 25 December 1941–2 January 1942. The Pacific Fleet was inactive, due to the Non-Aggression Pact with Japan concluded on 13 April 1941.

Baltic Fleet, 1941: officers in the conning tower of an M28 *Dekabrist* ('Decembrist') class submarine. They wear officers' M24 black rubberized raincoats and protective headgear, the man at the right with aircrew goggles. (Tshakov Collection)

Naval Infantry

As Red Army losses steadily mounted under the Axis onslaught, naval personnel were diverted from sea-going duties from July 1941 to form Naval Infantry (*Morskaya Pekhota*) units to defend their bases. In addition, from 18 October 1941, 37 specialized Naval Infantry Rifle Brigades were formed.

A Naval Infantry Brigade (*Brigada Morskoi Pekhoti*), subordinated to a Fleet, was a scratch unit with a Brigade HQ, hardly any HQ Troops, and between three and seven numbered Naval Infantry battalions. Up to 31 December 1941, seven brigades were

Table 4: Red Army and Navy ranks and rank insignia, 3 December 1935–12 July 1940			
Land Force Combat Arms *(collar insignia/cuff chevrons)*	**Air Force Combat Arms** *(collar insignia/cuff chevrons)*	**Navy Combat Arms** Technical Officers (2) *(cuff rings & bars)*	**British Army/ Royal Navy 1939–1945**
Vysshiy komandniy sostav (Corps of Chief Commanders)			**General Officers**
Marshal Sovetskogo Soyuza *(large star/star wide gold & medium red)*	–	–	Field Marshal/ Admiral of the Fleet
Komandarm 1-go ranga *(star, 4 diamonds/star, wide gold)*	**Komandarm 1-go ranga** *(star, 4 diamonds/star wide gold)*	**Flagman Flota 1-go ranga** *(star, 3 medium 2 wide rings)*	(Senior) General/ (Senior) Admiral
Komandarm 2-go ranga *(4 diamonds/4 medium gold)*	**Komandarm 2-go ranga** *(4 diamonds/4 medium gold)*	**Flagman Flota 2-go ranga** Inzhener-flagman flota *(star, 3 medium 1 wide rings)*	General/ Admiral
Komkor *(3 diamonds/3 medium gold)*	**Komkor** *(3 diamonds/3 medium gold)*	**Flagman 1-go ranga** Inzhener-flagman 1-go ranga *(star, 2 medium 1 wide rings)*	Lieut-General/ Vice-Admiral
Komdiv *(2 diamonds/2 medium gold)*	**Komdiv** *(2 diamonds/2 medium gold)*	**Flagman 2-go ranga** Inzhener-flagman 2-go ranga *(star, 1 medium 1 wide rings)*	Major-General/ Rear-Admiral
Kombrig *(1 diamond/1 medium gold)*	**Kombrig** *(1 diamond/1 medium gold)*	**Kapitan 1-go ranga** (3) Inzhener-flagman 3-go ranga *(star, 1 wide ring)*	Brigadier/ Commodore
Starshiy komandniy sostav (Corps of Senior Commanders)			**Field officers**
Polkovnik *(3 bars/1 medium red edged gold)*	**Polkovnik** *(3 bars/1 medium red edged gold)*	**Kapitan 2-go ranga** Voeninzhener 1-go ranga *(star, 4 medium rings)*	Colonel/ Captain
Mayor *(2 bars/2 medium red)*	**Mayor** *(2 bars/2 medium red)*	**Kapitan 3-go ranga** Voeninzhener 2-go ranga *(star, 3 medium rings)*	Major/ Lieut. Commander
Kapitan *(1 bar/1 medium red)*	**Kapitan** *(1 bar/1 medium red)*	**Kapitan-leytenant** Voeninzhener 3-go ranga *(star, 1 narrow 2 medium rings)*	Captain/ Lieutenant
Sredniy komandniy sostav (Corps of Intermediate Commanders)			**Subalterns**
Starshiy Leytenant *(3 squares/3 narrow red chevrons)*	**Starshiy Leytenant** *(3 squares/3 narrow red)*	**Starshiy Leytenant** Voentekhnik 1-go ranga *(star, 2 medium rings)*	(Senior) Lieut./ (Senior) Sub-Lieut.
Leytenant *(2 squares/2 narrow red)*	**Leytenant** *(2 squares/2 narrow red)*	**Leytenant** Voentekhnik 2-go ranga *(star, 1 narrow 1 medium rings)*	Lieutenant/ Sub-Lieutenant
Mladshiy Leytenant (1) *(1 square/1 narrow red)*	**Mladshiy Leytenant** (1) *(1 square/1 narrow red)*	**Mladshiy Leytenant** (1) Mladshiy Voentekhnik *(star, 1 medium ring)*	2nd Lieutenant/ Acting Sub-Lieut.
Mladshiy komandniy sostav (Corps of Junior Commanders)			**NCOs**
Starshina *(4 triangles)*	**Starshina** *(4 triangles)*	**Starshina** *(star, 2 medium bars)*	Warrant Officer II/ Chief Petty Officer
Mladshiy Komvzvod *(3 triangles)*	**Mladshiy Komvzvod** *(3 triangles)*	–	Sergeant
Otdelyonniy Komandir *(2 triangles)*	**Otdelyonniy Komandir** *(2 triangles)*	**Otdelyonniy Komandir** *(star, 1 medium bar)*	Corporal/ Leading Seaman
Ryadovoy sostav (Corps of Privates)			**Men**
Krasnoarmeyets *(plain collar-patch)*	**Krasnoarmeyets** *(plain collar-patch)*	**Krasnoflotets** *(star)*	Private/ Ordinary Seaman

Notes:
(1) Introduced 20 August 1937.
(2) Technical officers are listed here, as some of their titles differ from the Red Army, Air Force and NKVD equivalents.
(3) Regarded as a field officer, not a general officer.

identified: 3rd, 4th and 6th in Red Banner Baltic Fleet, fighting around Tallinn, Leningrad and Lake Ladoga; 7th–9th in Black Sea Fleet, around Odessa and Sevastopol; and 12th defending Murmansk for Northern Fleet. These units wore black naval uniforms (see below) and infantry equipment, with the Fleet title on the seaman's cap ribbon but no special Naval Infantry badge.

A Naval Rifle Brigade (*Brigada Morskoi Strelkovy*) was organized like a Red Army infantry brigade, with a Brigade HQ; HQ Troops (signals, sub-machine gun, engineer, motor transport and medical companies); plus three infantry battalions, and light and heavy mortar, artillery and anti-tank battalions. Such brigades were under Red Army command and wore Red Army infantry uniforms. Two brigades (7th, 8th) are known to have fought on the Finnish front before the end of 1941.

An aircrew NCO of a Naval Aviation bomber squadron, his rank status identifiable by his M24 black service cap piped white and with M22 cap badge; he also wears a dark blue double-breasted thigh-length coat with a broad brown fleece collar. The bomb is inscribed 'A gift for Hitler'. (Nik Cornish Collection)

NAVY UNIFORMS

3 December 1935–13 July 1940

The VMF's M35 uniforms adopted from 3 December 1935 were developments of the M24 uniform, with an austere elegance reminiscent of the British Royal Navy. As in the Imperial Navy, many of whose traditions it retained, the principal uniform colour was black, with some dark blue and white items. The standard naval button was brass with a fouled anchor motif.

Naval officers' headgear was the M24 black worsted peaked service cap, with a black patent leather chin strap and peak, and a white cloth crown in summer. The crown and upper band edges were piped white; the M24 badge was a gold metal fouled anchor in a gold-embroidered wreath, below a red star edged gold and bearing a gold crossed hammer and sickle on a white disc. The officers' M24 black *pilotka* sidecap had white crown and flap piping, and a small peaked-cap badge. The M31 'Finnish' black lambskin cap with the service cap badge was worn in cold weather.

The officers' M35 black double-breasted, open-neck service jacket had two rows of four large gold front buttons, two rear cuff buttons, one internal left breast pocket without flap, and two internal waist pockets with buttonless square flaps; it was worn with a white shirt and black tie. The officers' M24 dark blue single-breasted everyday service tunic had a high closed standing collar, a straight sewn cuff with two rear buttons, five large gold front buttons, two internal breast pockets with buttonless scalloped flaps, and two internal waist pockets without flaps. The officers' M24 white cotton summer everyday service tunic had the same cut but only two patch breast pockets without flaps.

The officers' M24 black woollen greatcoat had a closed or open turn-down collar, two rows of five large gold buttons, two internal waist pockets with square buttonless flaps, and a buttoned rear half-belt. Their M24 black rubberized raincoat, worn with black rubberized protective headgear, had a closed turn-down collar, two rows of four plain black buttons, two patch waist pockets with square buttonless flaps, and a black rubberized belt with plain black buckle. Black trousers (white cotton in summer) and black leather shoes were also prescribed. All belts, pouches and holsters were black leather.

All non-commissioned ranks wore the 'square rig' seaman's uniform. Winter uniform for re-enlisted NCOs (ranking as *starshina* and *otdelyonniy komandir*) included the officers' M24 service cap with M22 badge, and a white cloth cover in summer. Conscripts wore the black M24 flat-topped *bezkozirka* seaman's cap with white piping to the crown and upper band edge, and a white cloth cover in summer; the M22 cap badge was worn on the front of the crown, above the name of the fleet, ship or establishment in gold capital letters on a black silk ribbon tally, with long, squared hanging ends bearing gold fouled anchors. They also had a black *pilotka* with white piping and the M22 badge.

The dark blue seaman's jumper had a wide blue collar with three white braid edgings, and shirt cuffs with two buttons, worn over a blue-and-white horizontally striped vest. The white cotton summer jumper had the blue collar, and blue cuffs with three white braid edgings and one button. A black belt had a brass rectangular buckle showing a fouled anchor; black or white trousers and black leather ankle-boots completed the uniforms.

The seamen's M24 black woollen double-breasted greatcoat had a closed turn-down collar, one row of functional buttons concealed by a fly on the right side, five large decorative brass front buttons, plain turnback cuffs, and two internal waist pockets with square buttonless flaps. In bad weather a double-breasted M24 black worsted *bushlat* pea-jacket was worn; this had a large turn-down collar, two rows of five large brass buttons, and two flapless internal side pockets in the lower chest. The fatigue uniform comprised a navy-blue beret with the M22 badge, and an off-white one-piece overall with an open turn-down collar (showing the striped vest), buttoned shirt cuffs, and a buttonless left breast patch pocket. Above the pocket a light grey tape bore the sailor's assignment in black numbering.

Branch distinctions

For officers, the branch was indicated by the badge above the cuff rank rings, the colours of rank rings and of cloth between them (or above and below single rings), and the colour of cap badges. Line officers had a gold embroidered cap badge, cuff star and braid rank rings: Seamen's branch plain, medical officers with dark brown cloth, Naval Aviation with light blue cloth (and Air Force qualification sleeve badges). Services and Specialist Officers had a silver embroidered cap badge, cuff star and braid rank rings: Supply and Administration plain, medical officers with green cloth, technical officers with crimson, legal officers with violet. Political officers had a gold cap badge, a red cuff star edged gold, and gold rank rings with red cloth. Naval technical general officers had different rank titles (see Table 4, note 2).

NCOs and sailors wore, on the left upper sleeve of the jumper and pea-jacket, red speciality badges

A Coastal Defence branch *kapitan 2-go ranga* commanding a Naval Infantry battalion. He wears the M24 black service cap, piped white, and dark blue everyday service tunic, with dark brown cloth identifying his branch between the cuff rank rings. His men have M24 *bezkozirka* caps or M40 helmets, M35 'square rig' uniforms, and infantry equipment. His high-collared tunic identifies a second officer, sitting bottom right. (Nik Cornish Collection)

on a black disc; these were ringed in gold or yellow for re-enlisted NCOs, and in red for conscripts. There were 25 specialities; some of the most common were, e.g., Boatswain, chained sea-anchor; Quartermaster (helmsman), ship's wheel; Rigger, seaman's knot; Fire Controlman, range-finder; Gunner, crossed cannons; Torpedoman, torpedo and cogwheel; Torpedo Electrician, torpedo and lightning bolts; Machinist, cogwheel and propeller; Electrician, lighthouse and lightning bolts; Ordnance Electrician, cannon and lightning bolts; Radio Operator, lightning bolts and anchor; Radio Technician, lightning bolts and 'whisker' wires; Telegraphist, long entwined lightning bolts; Signalman, crossed flags; and Storekeeper, unfouled anchor.

Autumn 1941: the six-man Naval Infantry crew of a 120mm M38 regimental mortar prepares to fire. All are wearing M40 helmets, M24 enlisted ranks' black greatcoats and black leather belt equipment, with slung M1891/30 rifles. (Nik Cornish Collection)

Rank insignia

The Navy introduced new cuff rank insignia (see Table 4) to replace the Imperial shoulder boards and Provisional Government cuff rings. Officers were styled 'commanders', but a *kapitan 1-go ranga* was a field grade officer, unlike the Army equivalent of *kombrig*. On the cuffs of the M35 black service jacket and greatcoat and M24 dark blue everyday service tunic, Seamen's branch officers wore a gold braid star above narrow (0.6cm), medium (1.3cm) and wide (3.2cm) gold braid rings. On the cuffs of the M24 white everyday service tunic and black rubberized raincoat they wore gold braid bars on uniform-colour patches. On the cuffs of the dark blue and white jumpers and the M24 black greatcoat and pea-jacket, NCOs and sailors wore a red cloth star and 2–0 red cloth bars.

NKVD SECURITY FORCES

The Soviet Union – a multinational totalitarian state, to which a large proportion of the population owed no political, national or ethnic allegiance – required a significant military and security apparatus to control its own citizens by force. The People's Commissariat for Internal Affairs (*Narodnyi Komissariat Vnutrennikh Del* – NKVD) was formed in 1918 to oversee state security. It was later commanded by two of the most infamous men in Soviet history: *General'niy Komissar GB* Nikolai Ivanovich Yezhov, 26 September 1936–25 November 1938, succeeded by *General'niy Komissar GB* Lavrentiy Pavlovich Beriya until 29 December 1945. The NKVD was divided in 1939 into 17 Chief Directorates: State Security; three administrative (Economics, Administration, Archives); Fire Brigades; Police (*Militsiya*); Internal Troops (ten Chief Directorates), and Border Troops. Of these, State Security, Internal and Border Troops will be considered here.

These forces wore M35 Red Army khaki uniforms, with NKVD rank insignia introduced 15 July 1937 for the service tunic, field shirt and greatcoat (see Table 5). Unlike the Red Army combat arms, however, officers did not wear gold collar-patch piping.

'The Poison Dwarf': the commander of the NKVD in 1936–38 was the 5ft-tall Nikolai Yezhov, an ultra-Stalinist who supervised the Great Purge. Despite his merciless zeal, Stalin, wary of his power, had Yezhov himself executed on 4 February 1940.

Yezhov wears the M35 GUGB khaki uniform with the M36 rank insignia of a *general'niy komissar GB* (superceded in July 1937 – see Note (1) in Table 5, opposite), with gold collar and cuff piping. The dark red collar patches, piped crimson and with a narrow gold central line, display a small M36 gold star edged with blue and bearing a red hammer and sickle. On the upper sleeve is the GUGB general officer's badge, and above the cuffs a larger version of the collar-patch star above a gold braid bar. (Tshakov Collection)

State Security

The State Security Main Directorate (*Glavnoye Upravlenie Gosudarstvennoi Bezopasnosti* – GUGB) conducted espionage abroad, and within the USSR combated foreign spies, sabotage and terrorism, eliminated 'anti-Soviet' organizations, monitored Communist ideology amongst the population (especially hostile minorities), and guarded senior party and government officials. The GUGB was briefly separated from 3 February 1941 to form its own People's Commissariat (NKGB), but returned to NKVD control on 20 July 1941. The GUGB commanders were *Komkor* Mikhail Frinovsky, 15 April 1937; *Komissar GB 1-go ranga* Lavrentiy Beriya, 8 September 1938; and *Komissar 3-go ranga* Vsevolod Nikolayevich Merkulov, 25 November 1938.

GUGB officers wore dark red facings and crimson piping on all uniforms. Their most distinctive item was the dark blue NKVD service cap with a dark red band, and crimson piping to the crown and upper band edge. On all uniforms the *General'niy Komissar GB* wore dark red rhomboidal collar patches with gold upper edge piping and crimson lower edge piping, and a gold embroidered hammer and sickle on a large gold star edged light blue; this star was repeated on the cuffs. Other GUGB officers had distinctive rank titles emphasizing their relative seniority to Red Army ranks: e.g., a *kapitan GB* was equivalent to a Red Army *polkovnik*. They wore M35 Red Army rank badges on dark red collar patches edged crimson, but they had no cuff rank insignia. On both upper sleeves officers wore a dark red cloth oval badge; for general officers this bore a silver embroidered hammer, sickle and sword within a gold oval, and for other officers a gold embroidered hammer, sickle and sword hilt, the sword blade and oval edging being silver.

NKVD Internal Troops

The Chief Directorate for Border and Internal Troops (GUPVV) was formed on 29 September 1938, and divided into separate Chief Directorates on 8 March 1939. Under *Komdiv* (*Komkor*, 4 March 1940; *General-Leytenant*, June 1940) Ivan Ivanovich Maslennikov, the Internal Troops (*Vnutrenniye Voiska*) were administered by ten Chief Directorates: Transport, Prisons, Labour Camps (*Gulag*), Highways, Railway Security, Convoy Escort Troops, Factory Guards, Operational Troops, Military Provision and Military Construction.

NKVD Internal Troops units had always been organized on the Red Army model, but 30 NKVD Operational Divisions were formed 8 March 1939–31 December 1941, comprising six Motorized Divisions (1, 2, 11, 21–23), two Rifle Divisions (1, 4) and four Mountain Rifle Divisions (12, 15, 17, 26). In addition, Railway Security organized ten Railway Security Divisions (1, 3–10, 18); Factory Guards had four Special Installation Security Divisions (11, 12, 18, 25), and there were two Special Installation & Railway Security Divisions (19, 20). Finally, the Convoy Escort Troops formed two Convoy Troops Security Divisions (13, 14). Brutal and trigger-happy, the Internal Troops at least served some purpose in stiffening Red Army resistance to the Axis invaders.

All NKVD Internal Troops wore the dark blue NKVD peaked service cap, and M35 Red Army rank insignia and branch badges on dark red collar patches with crimson piping; combat-arm officers wore red and gold cuff chevrons, and political officers red cuff stars. There were units of infantry, cavalry, armour, motor transport, artillery, engineers, pontoon

Table 5: NKVD, Services and Specialist Officers' ranks and rank insignia, 3 December 1935–12 July 1940

NKVD GUGB State Security (collar insignia/cuff insignia) (1)	NKVD Operational & Frontier Troops (collar insignia/cuff chevrons) (1)	Red Army, Navy and NKVD Political Officers Supply & Administration/Medical/Veterinary/ Technical / Legal (1)	British Army/ Royal Navy 1939–1945
Vysshiy komandniy sostav (Corps of Chief Commanders) (2)			**General Officers**
General'niy Komissar GB (3) (large star/large star)	-	-	Field Marshal/ Admiral of the Fleet
Komissar GB 1-go ranga (star, 4 diamonds)	**Komandarm 1-go ranga** (star, 4 diamonds/star, wide gold)	**Armeyskiy Komissar 1-go ranga**	(Senior) General/ (Senior) Admiral
Komissar GB 2-go ranga (4 diamonds)	**Komandarm 2-go ranga** (4 diamonds/4 medium gold)	**Armeyskiy Komissar 2-go ranga** Armintendant/Armvrach/Vetarmvrach/ Arminzhener/Armvoenyurist (4)	General/ Admiral
Komissar GB 3-go ranga (3 diamonds)	**Komkor** (3 diamonds/3 medium gold)	**Korpusnoy Komissar** Korintendant/Korvrach/Vetkorvrach/ Korinzhener/Korvoenyurist (4)	Lieut-General/ Vice-Admiral
Starshiy major GB (2 diamonds)	**Komdiv** (2 diamonds/2 medium gold)	**Divizionniy Komissar** Divintendant/Divvrach/Vetdivvrach/ Kominzhener/Divvoenyurist	Major-General/ Rear-Admiral
Major GB (1 diamond)	**Kombrig** (1 diamond/1 medium gold)	**Brigadniy Komissar** Brigintendant/Brigvrach/Brigvetvrach/ Briginzhener/Brigvoenyurist	Brigadier/ Commodore
Starshiy komandniy sostav (Corps of Senior Commanders)			**Field Officers**
Kapitan GB (3 bars)	**Polkovnik** (3 bars/1 medium red edged gold)	**Polkovoy Komissar** Intendant, Voenvrach, Vetvoenvrach , Voeninzhener, Voenyurist ...1-go ranga	Colonel/ Captain
Starshiy Leytenant GB (2 bars)	**Mayor** (2 bars/2 medium red)	**Batal'onniy Komissar** Intendant, Voenvrach, Vetvoenvrach, Voenzhener, Voenyurist ...2-go ranga	Major/ Lieut. Commander
Leytenant GB (1 bar)	**Kapitan** (1 bar/1 medium red)	**Starshiy Politruk** Intendant, Voenvrach, Vetvoenvrach, Voenzhener, Voenyurist ...3-go ranga	Captain/ Lieutenant
Sredniy komandniy sostav (Corps of Intermediate Commanders)			**Subalterns**
Mladshiy Leytenant GB (3 squares)	**Starshiy Leytenant** (3 squares/3 narrow red)	**Politruk** Tekhintendant 1-go ranga/Starshiy Voenfel'dsher/Starshiy Vetvoenfel'dsher/ Voentekhnik 1-go ranga/Voenyurist	(Senior) Lieut./ (Senior) Sub-Lieut.
Serzhant GB (2 squares)	**Leytenant** (2 squares/2 narrow red)	**Mladshiy Politruk** Tekhintendant 2-go ranga/Voenfel'dsher/ Vetvoenfel'dsher/Voentekhnik 2-go ranga/ Mladshiy Voenyurist	Lieutenant/ Sub-Lieutenant
–	**Mladshiy Leytenant** (5) (1 square/1 narrow red)	- Mladshiy Voentekhnik (5)	2nd Lieutenant/ Acting Sub-Lieut.
Mladshiy komandniy sostav (Corps of Junior Commanders)			**NCOs**
–	**Starshina** (4 triangles)	**Zamestitel' Politruka** (6)	Warrant Officer II/ Chief Petty Officer
–	**Mladshiy Komvzvod** (3 triangles)	–	Sergeant
–	**Otdelyonniy Komandir** (2 triangles)	–	Corporal/ Leading Seaman
Ryadovoy sostav (Corps of Privates)			**Men**
–	**Krasnoarmeyets** (plain collar-patch)	–	Private/ Ordinary Seaman

Notes:
(1) NKVD badges of rank introduced 15 July 1937. The NKVD Naval Division and Coastguard had Red Navy ranks and rank insignia.
(2) Only NKVD GUGB, Internal and Frontier Troops were designated 'commanders'.
(3) GB = 'State Security' (Gosudarstvennoy Bezopasnosti).
(4) The NKVD had no Services or Specialist Officer ranks at this level.
(5) Introduced 20 August 1937, but not in the Red Navy.　　　(6) Introduced 5 April 1938.

engineers, electrical engineers, railway troops, construction engineers, signals, chemical troops, and air force (with dark blue *pilotka* caps), with all the appropriate branch badges worn on the collar patches. There were also Supply and Administration, Medical and Veterinary services, and technical, legal and bandmaster Specialist Officers (highest rank, *komdiv* equivalent). A Naval Division wore the full range of naval uniforms, branch and rank insignia.

NKVD Border Troops

The Border Troops (*Pogranichnyie Voiska*) became a separate Chief Directorate (GUPV) on 8 March 1939, under *Komandarm 1-go ranga* Grigoriy Grigorevich Sokolov. They were organized into ten Border Military Districts corresponding to Red Army Military Districts, each District (*Pogranichniy Okrug*) administering about 6,000 men in Border Regiments (total, about 50). A Border Regiment (*Pogranichniy Polk*) was divided into numbered Border Detachments (detachment = *Pogranotryad*).

Border units saw action at Khalkin-Gol, and participated in the Winter War. Border units on the Lithuanian, Byelorussian, Ukrainian and Moldavian frontiers bore the full brunt of the Axis invasion from 22 June 1941, suffering huge losses as they desperately defended the borders and cities of the Western Soviet Union.

NKVD Border Troops wore a green service cap with a dark blue band, piped crimson on the crown and band upper edge. All ranks wore M35 Red Army rank badges and, like the NKVD Internal Troops, the full range of branch badges including Air Force, Services, Specialist and Political officers, on green collar patches piped crimson. Combat-arm officers wore red and gold cuff chevrons, and Political Officers red cuff stars. Coastguard Patrol Boat Brigades wore naval uniforms and insignia.

PLATE COMMENTARIES

A: ARMED FORCES COMMANDERS, 1939

A1: *Marshal Sovetskogo Soyuza* Kliment Voroshilov
Appointed People's Commissar for Defence on 20 June 1934, Voroshilov wears the M35 officers' winter service uniform with the dark grey greatcoat and special red collar, cuff and front piping, and the distinctive large gold star on the rhomboidal collar patches of marshal's rank. He carries a holstered 7.62mm M1895 Nagant 'gas seal' revolver. This convinced Communist and Stalinist dragged the Red Army to humiliation in the Winter War, for which he was dismissed on 7 May 1940.

A2: *Flagman Flota 2-go ranga* Nikolai Kuznetzov
Kuznetzov typified the independent-minded professional officer still able to survive under Stalin's repressive regime, serving as People's Commissar for the Navy from 8 April 1939 to 25 February 1946 (when Stalin finally had him arrested on trumped-up charges). This austere black M24 naval officers' service jacket uniform was worn until May 1940, when more extravagant cap, collar and shoulder insignia were introduced.

A3: *Komandarm 2-go ranga* Aleksandr Loktionov
An Army officer, Loktionov served without distinction as Deputy People's Commissar for Aviation from December 1937 to September 1939; he was later arrested on false charges, and executed on 28 October 1941. He wears the M35 dark blue uniform marking the Air Force as an elite organization within the Red Army, with light blue collar patches, piping, and (although almost hidden by the badge) cap-badge backing star. The distinctive *pilotka* cap, dating back to the Imperial Air Service, was intended in 1935 as the only headgear, but Air Force officers lobbied for a peaked service cap, which was duly introduced in 1936. Note the pilot's 'wings' qualification badge on the left sleeve.

B: KHALKIN-GOL, AND COSSACKS, 1939

B1: *Komkor* Georgiy Zhukov, 1st Army Group; Khalkin-Gol, August 1939
Zhukov, perhaps the most talented and successful Soviet military leader of World War II, enjoyed his first victory at Khalkin-Gol. He wears the officers' M35 *French* tunic with infantry collar patches. His medals (ribbons were not yet worn on field uniform) are two Orders of the Red Banner for heroism or distinguished service, and the 20 Years' (Service) Medal.

B2: *Mladshiy Komvzvod*, 57th Rifle Division; Khalkin-Gol, June 1939
This platoon sergeant wears the M35 summer field uniform for NCOs and men, with an M38 *panama* field hat and light cotton field shirt and trousers. His field equipment includes the M35 enlisted belt with M38 light grey canvas supporting straps and M1917 rifle ammunition pouches, M38 backpack,

Summer 1941: an infantry *leytenant* waves his TT-33 pistol as he encourages his platoon to advance – the absence of a steel helmet suggests a posed photograph. He wears officers' M35 field uniform, with M41 khaki subdued collar patches with infantry branch badges. Unusually, the two shoulder braces of his M32 field equipment are worn crossed over his chest – under the gasmask bag sling – instead of vertical from hips to shoulders. (Tshakov Collection)

SM-1 gasmask in its bag, and a blanket roll over the left shoulder. He carries the standard Soviet rifle of the period, the 7.62mm M1891/30 Mosin Nagant, with socket bayonet.

B3: *Mladshiy Leytenant*, Kuban Cossacks; Northern Caucasus, 1939

Russian and Ukrainian Cossacks, fiercely loyal to the Tsars, had formed independent farmer-soldier communities in the Caucasus. They were repressed after the Civil War, but Cossack units were cautiously revived in the 1930s by a still-suspicious Soviet state that was nevertheless anxious to exploit their military skills in the unstable North Caucasus. This Kuban Cossack wears his regional variation on the traditional Cossack dress uniform, complete with sabre, whip, and *kindjal* dagger, and Red Army cavalry insignia.

C: EASTERN POLAND, SEPTEMBER 1939

C1: *Polkovnik*, 22nd Tank Brigade, Byelorussian Front

This regimental commander in 3rd Army, part of the occupation force sent into eastern Poland with Nazi agreement, wears the M35 'steel-grey' service dress that marked the Armoured Troops as an elite branch. The open-collar tunic has red piping, and officers' M35 collar-patch and cuff rank insignia. This

colonel wears the officers' service belt with the star buckle, often worn in the field against regulations, and a holstered 7.62mm Tula-Tokarev TT-30 or TT-33 semi-automatic pistol.

C2: Sniper, 81st Rifle Division, Ukrainian Front

This *Krasnoarmeyets* ('Red Army man') or infantry private of a 5th Army formation occupying eastern Poland would have encountered isolated but determined Polish resistance. He wears winter field uniform with the M36 steel helmet. Note the plain infantry-crimson collar patches (infantry had no branch badge until 1940), a branch-colour cloth strip on the front of his field shirt, and an unofficial belt buckle denoting his sniper status. He displays the Excellent Red Army Soldier and Sniper badges above his left breast pocket, and carries at his hip the case for the sniperscope of his M1891/30 rifle.

C3: *Starshina*, Red Banner Baltic Fleet

The Navy had only two non-commissioned or senior petty officer ranks between 22 December 1935 and 7 May 1940. Both wore the seaman's 'square rig' uniform with the black M35 enlisted peaked cap (identical to the officer's M24 except in quality), with the M22 cap badge. This chief petty officer has a dark blue jumper with red cuff rank insignia, and a wide dark blue seaman's collar with triple white edging braid (but no black neckerchief), worn over the blue-and-white striped vest; note the Excellent Red Army Soldier breast award. He wears black trousers, and the black leather enlisted ranks' belt with the seaman's buckle.

D: FINNISH-SOVIET 'WINTER WAR', 1939–40

D1: *Brigadniy Komissar*, 35th Tank Brigade; Mannerheim Line, December 1939

This brigade commissar, representing the Soviet Communist Party's powers within the Red Army, ranked equally with the brigade commander and, although not militarily trained, he had to countersign all the *kombrig's* orders. He wears Armoured Troops officers' field uniform, with a steel-grey *pilotka* sidecap and field shirt piped red; his commissar status is denoted by the red cuff star, and collar patches with enlisted men's red edging and no branch badge.

D2: *Otdelyonniy Komandir*, 44th Rifle Division; Suomussalmi, January 1940

The Red Army suffered its greatest defeat of the Winter War at Suomussalmi in east-central Finland, when Finnish infantry destroyed the Ukrainian 44th Rifle Division between 4 and 8 January, breaking it into small groups to be picked off individually. This infantry section commander wears the M27 mid-grey enlisted ranks' *budyonovka* field cap with ear flaps buttoned down, and the M27 enlisted greatcoat with infantry collar patches. His equipment includes the simple M39 backpack, waterbottle and entrenching tool. He is carrying the effective 7.62mm Degtyarov DP-28 section light machine gun.

D3: *Zamestnitel' politruka*, Air Force; Leningrad Military District, November 1939

The Deputy Political Officer, ranking as a *starshina*, was introduced from 5 April 1938, as Stalin's 'Great Purge' raged, to expand political control throughout the ranks of the Red Army. This senior NCO is wearing an Air Force M35 dark blue enlisted ranks' peaked field cap and greatcoat, khaki enlisted field shirt, and M38 field-belt, although a *starshina* could also wear an officers' belt. Political officers captured by the Germans often removed their cuff stars in hope of escaping summary execution under Hitler's 'Commissar Order'.

An infantry squad wearing khaki quilted *telogreika* overjackets and *vatnie sharovari* trousers. They are armed with the relatively unsuccessful Tokarev SVT-40 semi-automatic rifle with knife bayonet. (Nik Cornish Collection)

E: BALTIC STATES, 1940–41

E1: *Leytenant* of Cavalry, 22nd Territorial Corps; Estonia, September 1940

This former subaltern in the Estonian Cavalry Regiment, forcibly drafted into the Red Army, still wears the Estonian Army M36 peaked cap, belt and crossbrace, cavalry closed-collar tunic, silver-striped red breeches, boots, and sabre. Features added by his new masters are the Red Army M22 cap badge, and officer's collar and cuff rank insignia with cavalry branch distinctions. The Red Army rightly distrusted this second-line formation, many of whose personnel promptly (and understandably) deserted to the Germans in July 1941.

E2: *Starshina* of Armoured Troops, 5th Tank Division; Lithuania, June 1941

The 3rd Mechanized Corps, defending Lithuania, had been destroyed by July 1941. This NCO wears the M33 tank crew helmet and the blue overall over his M35 winter field shirt. Following regulations, he displays no rank insignia on his overall; on the *gymnastiorka* the M40 collar patches have the inner gold braid edging unique to this rank. As the senior company NCO, the *starshina* was a key man in the Red Army's otherwise weak NCO corps. He carries officers' binoculars and – since most Red Army tanks of this date had no radio – signalling flags.

E3: *Starshiy Mayor*, GUGB State Security; Tallinn, August 1941

This officer – who has been helping supervise the rounding up, deportation and execution of some 125,000 citizens of the Baltic states – wears the dark blue NKVD peaked service cap with dark red band and crimson piping; a general officers' light grey field shirt with crimson collar and cuff piping; dark red collar patches piped crimson, and GUGB general officers' sleeve badges. Note the coloured enamel M40 Excellent NKVD Soldier badge above his left breast pocket, and his TT-33 pistol. His dark blue service breeches are piped crimson.

F: BYELORUSSIA AND UKRAINE, 1941

F1: *Marshal Sovetskogo Soyuza* Semyon Timoshenko, July 1941

Timoshenko's reputation as a competent army commander was secured in Finland from January 1940, and he became People's Commissar for Defence in May 1940. Although dismissed by Stalin in July 1941 for the Red Army's failures in the face of the Axis invasion, Timoshenko continued to occupy senior staff and field commands. Here he wears the light grey M40 service cap and tunic of a Marshal of the Soviet Union, with bright red facings and pipings introduced on 13 July 1940 along with new collar and cuff rank insignia. His medals are Hero of the Soviet Union, two Orders of Lenin, three Orders of the Red Banner, and a 20 Years' Service Medal.

F2: *Kapitan*, NKVD Frontier Troops; Byelorussian Frontier District, June 1941

Although essentially part of the oppressive Soviet internal security apparatus, Border Troops fought courageously to defend the Soviet western frontier in June 1941. This Detachment commander wears the green service cap, Red Army officers' M35 field shirt with green collar patches piped crimson and bearing the M40 infantry branch badge, the cuff rank chevrons of the combat arms, and Excellent Red Army Soldier and silver sports badges. He wears M38 officers' field equipment, with an M32 brown leather belt and and webbing M38 holster, mapcase and supporting straps.

F3: *Krasnoflotets*, Naval Infantry, Black Sea Fleet; Sevastopol, November 1941

Sailors fighting as infantry defended Odessa, Sevastopol and the Ukrainian and Crimean coasts in 1941, their tenacity in battle earning them the nickname 'Black Death'. This 'Red sailor' is wearing the M35 'square rig' uniform, the ribbon of his *bezkozirka* cap showing *Chernomorskiy Flot* (Black Sea Fleet) in gold Cyrillic embroidery. He wears red cloth star cuff rank badges and the gunner's speciality badge on the sleeves of his *bushlat* pea-jacket. His belt, marching boots, and the M37 pouches for his M1891/30 rifle are black leather, and he carries a slung SM-1 gasmask bag.

G: WESTERN RUSSIA, 1941

G1: *Yefreytor* of Artillery, 108th Rifle Division; Smolensk Pocket, July 1941

This gunner, from 575th Field Artillery Regiment in a 16th Army formation, is trapped inside the Smolensk Pocket by

Naval infantrymen, in black M24 uniforms with pea-jackets, pose as if operating a 50-PM-39 light mortar. The mortarman shows a boatswain's red sleeve badge; his senior NCO in the background has a peaked service cap, binoculars, and RGD-33 stick grenades in his belt. (Tshakov Collection)

A medical officer (*Voenvrach 3-go ranga*) bids farewell to a young infantryman at a field hospital; the doctor has M41 collar patches without a branch badge. The men wear M40 fur caps and M35 greatcoats, the military nurse a white cap and overall. (Nik Cornish Collection)

German Army Group Centre. He wears the enlisted ranks' M35 *pilotka* sidecap and field shirt, with M40 artillery collar rank insignia. Typically, he carries minimal field equipment while serving his gun – an SM-1 gasmask bag and M38 field belt. 16th Army was disbanded on 8 August; this soldier would either have been killed, or taken prisoner – in which case his chances of survival were very little better – or might have escaped eastwards to Soviet lines.

G2: *Voenvrach 2-go ranga*, Medical Corps, 139th Rifle Division; Uman Pocket, August 1941

This medical battalion commander serves in a 24th Army division trapped in the Uman Pocket in central Ukraine. He wears the officers' M35 field uniform, but – as a services rather than a combat-arms officer – red collar-patch piping like the enlisted ranks, and no cuff rank insignia. As his division's plight becomes more desperate he goes out into the front lines himself, carrying a rifle, a medical orderly's first aid haversack, a large medical waterbottle and a map-case, and has donned a Red Cross armband.

G3: *Leytenant*, Northern Fleet; Rybachiy Peninsula, November 1941

The Karelian Front defended the Rybachiy Peninsula against German-Finnish forces advancing on the ice-free port of Murmansk – later to be the destination of Allied convoys carrying life-saving military aid to the Soviet Union. This junior naval officer is wearing the M31 'Finnish' black lambskin cap with M24 officers' badge; the M24 greatcoat with M40 rank insignia on cloth cuff patches; and officers' black leather field equipment, comprising a belt, two cartridge pouches, and a holster for his M1895 revolver with a black lanyard.

H: MOSCOW, DECEMBER 1941

H1: *Starshiy Leytenant* of Engineers, 173rd Mountain Rifle Division; Kashira

This formation in 33rd Army prevented 2. Panzerarmee from encircling Moscow from the south. This deputy commander of a divisional engineer company is wearing the officers' M35 winter uniform, with the M40 fur cap; the officers' M35 dark grey greatcoat over his field shirt, both with M40 engineer officer's collar patches and branch insignia. He has the

officers' M32 brown leather field equipment of belt, two shoulder braces, holster and mapcase.

H2: *Mladshiy Serzhant*, 11th Motorcycle Regiment, Kalinin Front

In all, 32 motorcycle regiments were formed in 1940, of which 30 were attached to mechanized corps – a type of formation that was deactivated in July 1941. The 11th Regiment was then attached to 30th Army of the Kalinin Front, which forced the exhausted 4. Panzerarmee back from Moscow in December 1941. This corporal, astride a TIZ-AM-600 motorcycle, is wearing the M40 steel helmet with goggles; the M41 quilted jacket (introduced 25 August 1941), with M40 Armoured Troops collar patches and Motorcycle branch badge. On his M38 field belt is a magazine pouch for his Degtyarov PPD-40 sub-machine gun.

H3: Air Force pilot, Moscow Anti-Air Defence Zone

This VVS officer, whose mission is perhap to fly an early-mark MiG or Yak monoplane against the Luftwaffe supporting the German 4. Panzerarmee, is wearing aircrew cold-weather flight clothing: a brown leather fur-lined flying helmet and gloves (note sheepskin wiping-pads), khaki winter flight overall with a large brown fur collar and lining, and black leather *valenki* boots with light khaki felt legs. Note that no rank or any other insignia are worn. His M32 officers' belt and crossbrace support a holstered TT-33 pistol and a mapcase, and he wears PL-3M parachute harness.

Summer 1941: an officer in a sidecar leads his platoon of PMZ-A-750 motorcycle combinations across a bridge. They wear M33 tank-crew helmets and M35 field uniform, with black Armoured Troops collar patches piped red with M40 Motorcycle branch badges. (Nik Cornish Collection)

INDEX